Driving
Mr Morecambe

Michael Fountain and Paul Jenkinson

authors
online

An Authors OnLine Book

Text Copyright © Michael Fountain and Paul Jenkinson 2013

Cover design by Paul Jenkinson ©

All rights reserved. No part of this publication may be reproduced, stored in a retrieval system, or transmitted in any form or by any means, electronic, mechanical, photocopy, recording or otherwise, without prior written permission of the copyright owner. Nor can it be circulated in any form of binding or cover other than that in which it is published and without similar condition including this condition being imposed on a subsequent purchaser.

British Library Cataloguing Publication Data.
A catalogue record for this book is available from the British Library

ISBN 978-0-7552-0732-9

Authors OnLine Ltd
19 The Cinques
Gamlingay, Sandy
Bedfordshire SG19 3NU
England

This book is also available in e-book format, details of which are available at www.authorsonline.co.uk

Dedicated to:

*The lovely memories of
Eric Morecambe O.B.E.*

and

My first grandchild, Thomas James Fountain.

Contents

Foreword By Gail Stuart vii

Foreword By Gary Morecambe ix

Timeline xi

Chapter 1 – A Brief History Of Me 1

Chapter 2 – Where It All Started 11

Chapter 3 – Driver For Hire 18

Chapter 4 – New Start 25

Chapter 5 – Rolling Along 31

Chapter 6 – In The Back 37

Chapter 7 – The BBC 46

Chapter 8 – The Bank Raids 51

Chapter 9 – The Bank Raid Memoirs 63

Chapter 10 – At Home With The Morecambes 78

Chapter 11 – Contribution To Comedy 85

Chapter 12 – It Must Be Fete 93

Chapter 13 – Perks and Peril 100

Chapter 14 – A Special Day 109

Chapter 15 – The Fisherman 122

Chapter 16 – Sons and Daughters... 129

Chapter 17 – Moving On.. 133

Chapter 18 – Tewkesbury – The Beginning Of The End 139

Chapter 19 – On Stage.. 145

Chapter 20 – Silence Is Not Golden.. 148

Chapter 21 – After Eric.. 152

Chapter 22 – A Star In My Own Lifetime................................. 157

Chapter 23 – Looking Back 163

Acknowledgements... 172

Foreword By Gail Stuart

Well, about time! I am so pleased that Paul has encouraged Mike to co-produce a book and very happy to be asked to write a Foreword.

I do not think there can be many photographs taken of Dad out and about in the '70s and early '80s that do not include Michael Fountain. And if you can't see him, he is probably standing just out of shot!

I sometimes marvel at the way my father managed to surround himself with people that were the perfect counterfoil to himself, Ernie, my mother and dear Mike.

Mike was ALWAYS calm, cheerful, unflappable and immaculate! There must have been many occasions when he was like the proverbial serene swan on the water. Remember, these were pre-sat. nav. times and I don't ever recall Mike having to stop and look at a map.

My father had a complete horror of being late, keeping people waiting, which is with me to this day. So arriving at a venue ridiculously early was not uncommon. Mike would calmly drive around the block several times or until he deemed it a more appropriate time to arrive. We were usually first in and last out!

It goes without saying that Mike has a great sense of humour and twinkle in the eye. That was essential if spending any time with our family. I think I might have been the source of a few laughs for both men during my teenage years. Mike did once let slip that he and Dad used to refer to me as the Mary Hopkin of Harpenden! This was because my hair and dress were like hers and I enjoyed nothing more than sitting in the back of the car with the window wide open, singing full throttle into the wind. I particularly remember my rendition of Silence is Golden by The Tremeloes. I am blushing at the memory. Especially that high chorus in their falsetto voices, "Silence is golden, golden but my eyes still see..." Oh, happy days!

I am sure that my Father and Mike had great mutual respect and a fondness for each other that the years must have fostered. You could say that Mike was a very lucky man to be Dad's chauffeur, able to observe him at such close quarters for so long. I am sure Dad would say that he was a very lucky man to have Mike as his driver, minder, props man and confidant, with him at the end.

I am expecting to have a tear in my eye and a smile on my face as I read this book about such a wonderful time with a wonderful man, by a wonderful chauffeur, known to us quite simply as, "Mike the Driver".

Gail Stuart

Foreword By Gary Morecambe

I was so thrilled when Paul Jenkinson told me that, after all these years – nearly three decades of them since my father's death – he was working with Mike Fountain on a memoir of his many years driving my father all over the country.

I was about twelve when I first met Mike, and while his job was to drive Eric Morecambe to the studios and back mostly, my job was to drive Mike round the bend! At least that's the way I saw it, and I'm sure at times I succeeded. One occasion I have in mind is when Mike was preparing to drive Eric to a function late one afternoon and he came over to the swimming pool, which I was in at that moment. He looked so suave in his chauffeur's suit and cap that I just had to do a bomb in the water and soak him. That was possibly the most angry I ever saw him. "Look what you've done to my suit!" he shouted – but that was it. And that was the first sign, and no doubt reason why I recall it so vividly, of his wonderfully tolerant nature. He was always patient beyond the call of duty, even to a miserable horror of a twelve-year-old!

The fact that in my own late middle age we can still meet up for a meal and a few laughs and reminisce says it all really – it says he must be senile!

Actually, and in all honesty, what it says is that there is no stronger bond than a shared journey – and that is somewhat appropriate bearing in mind Mike's former job description. Talking of which makes me recall very clearly that Mike was anything but Eric's chauffeur. Well, he was that of course, but what I mean is he quickly became much more – he was the Mister Fixit of the family, which if you ever saw my father try to do anything practical around the house you can understand how that soon came about.

Mike became gardener, electrician, general repairman and driver to my sister and self. I particularly recall school runs and airport visits – vivid being the airport visit memories; of how we would stand at the top of the car park at Heathrow (as you once could pre-terrorism) passing hours away with a sandwich and mug of soup watching those aircraft soar to warmer climes. And he became the third member of the Morecambe and Wise touring act. Indeed, he built up quite a relationship with Charlie the vent. doll, and recently I was able to reunite them on a return visit to Morecambe with Charlie to publicise work on the plan for a permanent museum in Eric's name.

I wish Mike and Paul all the best with this book. I thank Paul for doing such a wonderful job in helping to keep M&W out there in the ether world via his website with Gideon, and I thank Mike for his lifelong friendship, which has meant much more to me that he can ever realise.

You're in the driver's seat next time I'm up Morecambe way, Mike!

Gary Morecambe

Timeline

This timeline provides dates for television shows and events to allow comparison to the narrative in the book. It is by no means comprehensive and is meant solely to accompany the stories and events in this publication.

1925 – Ernest Wiseman born (hereafter known as Ernie).
1926 – John Eric Bartholomew born (hereafter known as Eric).

1939 – World War II starts.
1940 – Eric and Ernie first meet during an audition in Manchester.
1941 – Eric and Ernie perform for the first time as a double act.
1942 – Michael Fountain born (hereafter known as Mike).
1943 – Ernie called up to the Merchant Navy.
1944 – Eric becomes a Bevin boy.
1945 – World War II ends.
194? – Eric and Ernie meet by chance in London and restart the act.

1953 – Eric's daughter Gail is born.
1954 – Running Wild (first television series). Broadcast on the BBC and considered a disaster.
1956 – Eric's son Gary is born.

1961 – Two Of A Kind (series 1). New TV series for ATV that would run for 7 years.
1962 – Two Of A Kind (series 2).
1963 – Mike left the Post Office to become a driver.
1963 – Two Of A Kind (series 3).
1963 – Mike becomes part-owner of the company.
1964 – Two Of A Kind (series 4).
1966 – Two Of A Kind (series 5).
1967 – Two Of A Kind (series 6) –the last of the ATV shows.
1969 – Eric and Ernie move from ATV to the BBC.
1969 – Morecambe & Wise Show series 1.
1969 – Eric suffers first heart attack.
1969 – The BBC employs Mike to drive Eric around for 12 months.

1970 – Eddie Braben becomes their writer as Sid Green and Dick Hills go back to ATV.
1970 – Mike becomes Eric's chauffeur.
1972 – Eric buys his first Rolls Royce.
1973 – Eric and Joan adopt Steven.
1974 – Eric gets his second Rolls Royce.
1976 – Eric and Ernie are awarded the O.B.E.
1977 – The Morecambe & Wise Show gets over 28 million viewers.
1978 – Eric and Ernie move from the BBC to Thames Television.
1979 – Eric suffers second heart attack.

1981 – Mike suffers minor heart attack.
1981 – Mike marries Lesley.
1984 – Eric collapses at Tewkesbury and dies.

1999 – Ernie dies.
1999 – Statue of Eric unveiled in Morecambe.
2010 – Statue of Ernie unveiled in Morley, Leeds.

Chapter 1 – A Brief History Of Me

The name Mike Fountain probably doesn't mean a lot to you unless you are an ardent fan of Morecambe and Wise. Even then you may be hard pushed to place the name in amongst the plethora of names that surrounded Britain's most loved double act. Shirley Bassey, André Previn, Cliff Richard, Angela Rippon; it's no surprise then you may not know me. My name is important to me though; I've had it since I was born.

For over fifteen years I was the personal chauffeur and friend of Eric Morecambe, or as the public like to be reminded, the one with the glasses. It was me who drove the famous Rolls Royce with the instantly recognisable number plate of EM 100 and it was me who drove Eric, and often his family, all over the UK, to rehearsals, shows, openings, trips, shopping and more. In fact if you were lucky enough to have ever spotted that beautiful car, odds are that the handsome chap in the front with the nice hat was me.

I have been many things in my life, mushroom grower, postman, store owner, but my time with Eric is the one I am most proud of and the one I would like to share with you. The happy times, when laughter flooded around the car with Eric, still switched on from a previous performance, bombarding me with jokes and one-liners. The memorable times like his visit to Silverstone, the day he was glad to be wearing brown trousers. The time he saved my life, and of course the sad and touching times that even now brings tears to my eyes as I recall those events and feelings.

When you work for someone as closely as I did, you get to know the man, the real man, and through this book I hope to share some of that person the public never got to see. Before we delve into the life and times of the comedic genius though, I thought it might interest you to learn a little about me and where I came from.

It was 1942, July to be exact, the 24th if you want the details, when I decided that the world was ready for me, or rather I was ready for the world. My parents Hyla and Constance agreed, and so like millions of other babies I emerged into this world kicking and screaming in the Red House Hospital Harpenden. My first home was 'The Cabin', not as glorious as the name suggests, it was a small house on Townsend Lane, Harpenden. Next-door but one was the Glen Eagle Hotel, and there are pictures of me somewhere being cradled by the head chef at the time.

Harpenden was more of a village then, and my parents had moved there because my father had just got a new job as an insurance agent, having previously been employed in the upholstery business. My life in 'The Cabin' is pretty much a blank. I lived there for only two years, and so any memories I have, are in fact what I gleaned from my parents later on in life.

The one thing that was always talked about, and dragged up to embarrass me at every opportunity, was my encounter with food during the bombing of Skew Bridge in Harpenden. As with many families, once the siren went off, if you didn't have a shelter or time to get to one, you just sat under the kitchen table and hoped for the best.

As a two-year-old though, this was more like a game to me, and my mother recounts this one particular occasion as we sat there waiting for the bombs to hit and hoping it wouldn't break our table.

I was crouched next to her, unaware of the terror she was feeling and entertaining myself with some jars of treacle. Rolling them about, stacking them up, knocking them down, building pyramids; to a child a few jars can become anything. In my enthusiasm for my newfound toys, and out of sight of my mother, I managed to somehow remove all the lids. Great, now I had more toys... I wonder what this sticky stuff is? It was too late by the time my mother had noticed and she probably caught the smell before she actually saw it. Turning round she stared at me, powerless to move because of the air raid, furious and scared at the same time. There I sat, broad grin on my face, excited at what I had created and loving the nice warm feeling. I was covered from head to toe in thick treacle. Hands still clasped around a jar above my head, getting the last remaining gloops out as I chuckled and laughed. It was a brilliant new game and such a nice feeling.

My poor mother. Not only did she have the war to worry about, the bombs and the kitchen table, but now all her treacle was slowly running down my soggy clothes and on to the floor. In those days things were rationed too, so I can only imagine her exasperation. It was almost like a sketch from Morecambe and Wise, who at this time I had never even heard of.

We survived that bombing and several more, even the kitchen table made it through as I recall. After two years we moved to what would be my home for the next twenty plus years. The move itself didn't seem to have dampened my spirit for unusual games and I still managed to get up to the strangest of things.

I was once caught sitting in the middle of the busy A6, the main road from Luton to Harpenden. All it took to catch my attention was the previous night's rain and a missing catseye. This combination had created a nice little puddle, which I found irresistible, blinkering me from the dangers. I meandered into the road, stick in hand, oblivious of the swerving cars and angry drivers and sat down. It was great fun, thrashing at the water as hard as I could, seeing how big of a splash I could make and trying my best not to stay dry. Another damp game I had managed to create!

Onlookers began to shout as the cars and buses hurtled past, in the middle of it all was me, still trying to batter the puddle into submission. A neighbour heard the commotion and knowing my previous form immediately knew it was me. I must have had some kind of reputation for trouble, but he bravely waved the traffic aside and dragged me to safety. No harm done, no cars were damaged and although soaking wet, my clothes would easily dry. I never could find that stick again and I still get pleasure from driving over catseyes today. Strange how things stick with you.

My new home was 83 Luton Road, Harpenden, a large, nine-roomed Victorian house, with two bay windows that my Grandfather had bought for £500 in 1944. He got the rest of the house free! He was a sort of all year round Father Christmas; a very jolly man over 6'4" tall and 18 stone. I remember his well-rounded reddish face, bushy eyebrows and the hairs coming out of his ears fascinated me. He loved Guinness, his pipe and his two Airedale dogs. The house had an outside toilet and an indoor coalhouse. Where is the logic in that!

Summer was fine, but in winter the water was always frozen and the infamously stiff and shiny Izal toilet paper had to be snapped off before use. A softer option would be cut up newspaper, but that always left you with yesterday's news imprinted on your nether regions. We didn't have modern appliances, no fridge or freezer, instead we had a walk-in larder. Thick walls and marble shelves, no windows and a good solid door meant the food was always kept cool, and the lack of preservatives and additives meant it stayed fresh longer.

The house was sullenly decorated and the drab carpets were restricted to small squares in the middle of the room with a wide boarder of lino or wood around the edges. This acted as a stark wake-up call once your bare feet touched down on that. Who needed coffee when you had ice-cold floorboards in January?

Despite rationing we ate quite well, my favourite being Sunday when the family sat down to a proper Sunday lunch with roast beef. The remaining meat was carefully portioned to be used for the rest of the week, so other meals would include cold beef with mashed potatoes, minced beef and anything else that could be cobbled together from beef in different stages of shredding.

The family was close geographically as well as emotionally. My mother's father, Granddad Frank Graves lived with us, his wife Lillie having died a year after I was born. My dad's mother, Grandma

Sophia lived in Luton with her sister after her husband, and my grandfather John Fountain died in 1937. Granddad Frank lived with us until 1951 when he passed away on my father's birthday.

I often visited Sophia, more frequently when my father had to go to the office in Luton. Her house was a typical grandparents house, stuck in time and a child's exploration dream. Your imagination just ran riot, it was like visiting your very own private theme park.

The house itself was cosy; well one room was because it was the only one with heating. It had a large fireplace with a real fire, comfortable chairs and a good solid table. The other rooms all seemed to have curious and posh names, some only ever getting used for Christmas or funerals. These rooms were sombre, seemingly dark and unwelcoming, which made it even more exciting to explore them.

The kitchen was different though, and I always enjoyed going in and looking around. A large, blackened stove sat on one wall, close by a sink with a solitary tap. No hot water back then, so the stove was almost constantly lit and hot, if not for cooking then to heat water for cooking or the dreaded weekly bath.

Once old enough my school life started. I enjoyed it but never really excelled in anything. The teachers I remember could easily become characters in a sitcom, and I can recall them vividly.

Mr. Davies, a frustrated cricketer, at least I think so because he used to throw things at you if he caught you talking. Blackboard rubbers, chalk, books, anything that came to hand, there was no human rights back then, just good old-fashioned discipline. Mr. Ravasio, the cheek pincher. He would clasp your cheek between his thumb and finger and drag you from your desk to the front of the class. That really hurt both physically and emotionally. Mr. 'Beaky' Bloxham, the happy caner. He had a large nose and was a happy kind of man. He always smiled when he gave you the cane. Miss. Rumble, the eccentric music teacher. Mr. Jones the short-tempered Welshman and Mr. Hall, the history teacher that taught drama and played cricket.

A main event in the village was the touring cinema. A man arrived with a huge white screen, projector and rolls of film and set up an impromptu cinema in the scout hut. All of the kids were excited to see what new films he had brought, so excited that any remote thought of danger, if not already gone, was soon vanquished. Heading off on my bike I hurtled along the road, my head swimming with heroes and villains.

The road was on a hillside with a steep bank on one side that often shed pebbles and rocks on to the road especially after heavy rain. This was one such day and instead of being more careful, it suddenly became a challenge. I swerved around them paying little attention to anything but the next rock when suddenly the bike slipped from under me. Sprawling out I got to see the pebbles a bit closer than I wanted to but luckily kind onlookers were quickly on the scene.

I was gathered up and taken to someone's house and found myself surrounded by concerned women brushing the dirt from my legs and mopping up the blood. No one knew who I was but they guessed I was from the village and the only person in the village with a telephone was the butcher.

"We have a young lad here, riding like a madman on his bike. He's taken fall."

"Ah, that will be Michael. I'll tell his mother."

He went to my parents' house and told them of my accident and I was soon home safe and sound. I still have the scars on my legs but that was not my last encounter with a bicycle.

Eager to get home for lunch one day, I unhitched my bike and headed off towards my house. The other school children all stared at me.

"Oi, Mike, where are you going?"

"Home," I yelled back, "for dinner."

None of them said anything, they all just laughed. Undeterred I peddled home and arrived in one piece this time, walking into the kitchen to be met by my mother.

"What are you doing home?" she asked, looking worried and confused at the same time.

"Dinner," I said.

"But it's only ten o'clock!"

I had to ride back to school and face the laughs from the school. I have no idea why I thought it was lunchtime, I was just hungry and the bell had sounded for playtime, I was only a few hours out. It seems bicycles played a large part in my life and continued to do so even after I left school.

Life wasn't all play and learning though, like most children I had small jobs to earn a few pennies for sweets or pop. Pop, for those either too young or from the southern regions of England, was the name given to fizzy drinks like cola or lemonade. These small jobs were a way of teaching kids the value of things by making you work for them.

One such job was delivery boy. Something must have stuck because I've been delivering things on and off ever since. Strange how these little things can leave a lasting impression and subliminally guide your future life – or is that a bit too deep? This first delivery role however was not so prestigious as my future role, and the one this book will, eventually, go on to explain. Instead it involved a more sobering mode of transport, a bicycle.

Close to my house was a row of shops consisting of the usual village suppliers; butcher, greengrocer, haberdashery and a post office. The post office also sold paraffin by the gallon and vinegar by the pint, just be careful you didn't get them mixed up.

The bicycle was specially made and had a huge wire basket on the front that would be loaded up with orders that had to be taken to the customers. As a young fit boy, it was my job to get those supplies there, which for the most part, was enjoyable and easy. When the snow came though, it was a different proposition, and hauling a bike, laden with food, up a steep hill through snow was hard work. The more we struggled forward, the more we fell over. The more we fell over the more we laughed until eventually we reached the farmhouse, exhausted from giggling but proud to have complete our job. There seems to be a running theme here, yet another instance of me and wet clothes. It hadn't struck me before, maybe that explains a few things!

The grocer, Mr. Snuggs, taught me how to cut up a side of bacon, how to carve ham from the bone and how to cut cheese correctly. It is sad that these small, family run shops are disappearing, to be replaced by large supermarkets. These skills served me well when I left school, with below average reports and grades. With the experience I somehow got a job with International Stores. That was a big deal back then; International Stores were the first large supermarket chain with stores and shops everywhere. My role was Under Manager and unlike the shop assistants of today I had to be sent on courses to learn how to do things properly. I learnt how to carve ham in the right way, how to cut cheese, how fruit was to be stored, where certain foods came from and how they were prepared. But that was in the future, for now I was still a child.

Even though I was now getting older, I still had a mischievous streak. Along with some friends, I remember carefully threading some string through a row of letter boxes. In those days letter boxes had little knockers on the outside, just right for string. With all the houses linked we hid behind some hedges and tugged. As the string pulled through, each knocker dropped emulating a knock at the door. How we giggled when six or seven people all appeared at the door at the same time. Each looking suspiciously at their neighbour before tutting loudly and walking back inside.

My knack of getting into trouble didn't diminish as I grew older, things just got bigger and more dangerous. My friends the Collinson brothers, Roy Bunyon, John Cox and Wesley Maddy were typical adventurous kids. With no health and safety to get in the way of fun, we made our own rules but didn't always get the results we were expecting!

Building a den seemed like a good idea at the time, although it didn't strike us as dangerous to build it between a railway bridge and the banking of the A6. If this in itself didn't seem dangerous enough, we decided it was a bit dark inside, and thought a few candles would be the solution. Considering the entire den was built from dry wood, cardboard, branches and grass, looking back this somehow doesn't seem quite such a good idea.

At first things were great. The den was much brighter and much warmer and we all sat there proud of our great engineering achievement. I don't know if someone knocked over a candle, or the wax dripped, but it wasn't long before the floor was smouldering beneath us. As excited children we didn't even start to try and put it out, we just clambered over each other in a bid for freedom. By the time it was fully ablaze, we had all scarpered of course, in different directions. Not out of some clever plan to avoid being caught, but in sheer panic. The excitement of our new den had completely vanished and we were now, in our minds, criminals.

I scrambled down the bank, across an old disused badminton court and down a back alley, finally emerging on the main road. Scruffy, dirty, smelling of smoke and gasping for breath I suddenly came face-to-face with two policemen. Crumbs! The game is up and I'll be put in prison! Luckily they were in a hurry and didn't stop to consider I might be guilty of something. Apparently some idiot had set fire to a bridge and they were far too busy trying to get to the scene to worry about a boy who looked like a character from Oliver. Now the excitement came back. I had got away with it; I hadn't been caught and now had something to brag about in school. Apparently I was a hero, at least until someone else did something daring, or just as daft.

Thick choking smoke seemed to hold a fascination for us youngsters, much to the disgust of my mother, who would ultimately have to clean me and my clothes. A trick we liked to do was to stand on a railway bridge. At first it may not seem exciting or dangerous, but remember this was in the fifties. In those days the trains were still steam driven, and what could be more fun than standing on a bridge as a steam train passed beneath. The dirt and soot from the funnel engulfed us, much to our delight. Our clothes and bodies would end up covered in black soot, but we didn't care. We knew we were in for a scolding and a hard scrubbing when we got back, but it was worth it.

I continued to live at Luton Road right into early adulthood. My mother passed away in that house after suffering a stroke in 1961; she was only 42 years old. She had been unwell and on medication for years, but it still was shock for her to go so early in life. Eighteen months later and my father asked me frankly if I would mind if he brought another woman to the house. I had no objections, mainly because I knew her and it would mean less work for me to do. Father and Amy married within twelve months and I was the best man at my own father's wedding.

As all this was happening, two popular radio comedians were making a big stir and about to try their hand at television. I still hadn't heard of Morecambe and Wise, despite their rising fame as top radio funsters, and the disastrous *Running Wild* would make sure it stayed that way, at least for a little while longer.

Running Wild was Eric and Ernie's first attempt at their own television show in 1954, which collapsed in a heap of criticism from the press. Stock scriptwriters failed to catch the sparkle and the series crashed, sending the boys back to variety for many years.

I had no idea of course that our paths would cross; my thoughts were taken up with football, comics and with an ever growing frequency, girls. The lives of two radio celebrities that had been treading the boards for over ten years, while I was setting fire to things and finding new ways to get wet, didn't even register.

Chapter 2 – Where It All Started

The first steps to becoming a professional driver for me began in 1963 when I was working as a postman in Harpenden. The very same Harpenden that Eric had recently moved to and settled down with his family. By now he was married and had two children, Gail and Gary. In stark contrast to my paltry existence, Morecambe and Wise were topping the ratings on television with ATV, starring in their own show, *Two Of A Kind*. They had worked their way up and were now reaping the rewards of three successful series, with many more to go.

Back to reality and the normal man on the street, literally. I was scraping a living pushing envelopes and parcels through people's letter boxes. Climbing out of bed at 4:15 in the morning through all weathers, six days a week. I was still finding new ways of getting wet but by now it wasn't so exciting. No wonder I hadn't really seen Eric Morecambe on the television, I didn't get much time to do anything other than stomp about Harpenden in the early hours and sleep.

A good friend of mine and fellow postman, Charlie Thomas, had his own little sideline to make a few extra pennies. In those austere times you made your money any way you could and he was making his by being a part-time driver for a local car hire company. If they needed a driver at short notice, Charlie would step in, pick up and drop off customers and make a few bob in the process.

One day he approached me and made me an offer I couldn't refuse. I couldn't refuse because he was standing on my foot at the time and made a very convincing case for the pain to stop.

"We're a bit short." He said, his foot still planted firmly on mine.

"No we're not," I replied, trying to be funny, "we're the same height."

Yes times may have been hard but we still laughed. Charlie though didn't give up easily, after all, he was a postman and he wasn't about to let me get away. What he was trying, and successfully doing, by clever placement of pressure on my foot, was persuading me to help him out. I had never done anything like that before and thought that you needed special training or rigorous courses. Surely any Tom, Dick or Harry couldn't just jump into a car and call himself a professional driver? It seemed however, I was wrong, at least according to Charlie.

I argued with myself for some time, which is something I do a lot these days. What would it involve? How do you learn? Would this pain in my foot go away soon? Would it affect my driving if it didn't? Like all forms of work and all aspects of life, it all boils down to experience and a little bit of luck. What is chauffeuring? To be honest it is only driving a big car, looking after your client, having good road sense and wearing a nice hat.

With Charlie still standing on my foot, I decided to do the correct and decent thing, panic! Sadly that didn't stop him and so another idea quickly came to mind, I agreed. That seemed to do the trick, however I had now agreed to something I knew nothing about. They say nothing ventured, nothing gained, but I have no idea who 'they' are, or whether they said it whilst considering taking up driving as an occupation. It was that very saying that tipped the balance. Still keeping my normal and important job of postman and giving the dogs someone to chase, I decided to give professional driving a try as an extra little earner.

It was surprisingly easy to pick up, and besides, the extra money would come in handy to buy some new shoes now that one of mine had been flattened by Charlie. It was an exciting time. I drove beautiful cars, cars of distinction that turned heads as they glided past. I drove for weddings, funerals and a host of other functions for a host of different people. It was me, hardly recognisable, sat in the front, smooth and professional, in my chauffeur's uniform and hat.

What I didn't realise though was the other side of being a chauffeur; the hard work involved in keeping the cars running and looking their best. The very late nights, the tipsy passengers with no sense of time, and the effort involved in keeping your cool. Washing, cleaning, polishing and petrol, all part of the job, it wasn't all glamour. Of those chores in particular, petrol is a very important one as we are later to find out.

Several months had passed without incident and all the time I was gaining experience. All that was needed now was that little bit of luck to make the saying come true, and we didn't have long to wait. The owner of the hire company announced one day that he was thinking of retiring. With this in mind he said he was looking for someone to possibly take over the job when he finally turned in his keys. Something inside pushed me forward. A little voice said, "Step forward Mike Fountain" and for once it wasn't the rent man. He needed someone he knew and trusted, someone who could drive, someone professional and someone with a nice hat. Step forward a slightly nervous Mike Fountain, still saying to myself quietly, nothing ventured, nothing gained.

It would mean leaving behind the post office and driving full-time, with a view to take over the company when the owner moved on. Again I had the arguments with myself. Could I really leave the post office? Could I do it? Who would the dogs chase and would I find a nicer way to get wet? Although I wasn't too bothered about the business side of things, it was the wage that I found more attractive, that and the fact I wouldn't have to get up at 4:15 every morning.

Being a postman had its good points, mainly when it wasn't raining and all the neighbourhood dogs were locked inside, but having the chance of being a full-time professional chauffeur was too good to turn down. After a lot of deliberating I finally decided to let go of my mail sack, grab a firm hold of those car keys and see where they took me. It was a brave move but one I never regretted, at least that is, after the initial few weeks of trauma that normally comes with any new job.

As time passed the owner did eventually retire and I went into partnership with another fellow who quite by coincidence, came from Lancashire, the place where Eric was born. We each put our money in and took over the complete business. I was on top of the world; it seemed my life was at last moving in the right direction. From postman to driver, from driver to part-owner; step forward a slightly more confident Mike Fountain.

The new joint business was run from my home, or at least half of it. The Victorian house on Luton Road I had lived in since I was two was converted by my father into two flats. The ground floor was the business and the other two upper floors were lived in by my father and stepmother. This worked out really well, especially when myself and the other driver were out. In the days of no mobile phones or even answering machines, an unanswered call could mean lost business. My stepmother Amy was always on hand, taking the calls and keeping the business rolling in the right direction while we drove ourselves to exhaustion.

Being a residential area the cars had to be parked just around the corner in the street. With no parking restrictions like today, we had no trouble finding a place and leaving them there knowing we wouldn't get a ticket or they would be stolen or set on fire. We did have competition in the area, so we would have to fight for customers. In fact one rival company actually changed their name to A.A.B. Cars, just so they were first in the telephone directory. Strange name for a bloke!

As soon as we were up and running the gloss soon faded and the hard work began. We sat down to work out what we would do with the business. What we would need, how we would pay for it and how we could use whatever it was to make us more successful. We couldn't buy any new cars that we badly needed because we simply had no money. All of our joint cash had gone into buying the business leaving us with just the three original cars that came with the deal. We didn't even have the cash to put petrol in all of them!

Although old, the three cars had been well looked after and were in great condition. They were a black Ford Zephyr 6, a blue Ford Zephyr 4 and a black Austin Princess. Much of the early days were spent cleaning and polishing them, waiting for a job to come in. I'm surprised we didn't rub all the paint off! It was fun for a while and we traded jokes and jibes while dodging hastily thrown sponges.

"You've missed a bit there mate!" I shouted, ducking quickly and waiting for the wet cloth to fly past.

"You know what," he replied, "I'm bored of this. I think I'll... wash a car! That will be a nice change."

Yes we had a lot of spare time! We also had another car there, but we couldn't use it. It belonged to the previous owner and was lurking in the background waiting to be sold. What a hire car it would have made though. A 1938 Rolls Royce Limo in beautiful condition, I should know, I spent a lot of time cleaning it. The asking price was £500, not a lot you might think, but this was in the 60s. In today's prices that would be something like £7,000. Even so, it was still a bargain for such a prestigious car and I wanted it badly. We saved and saved but sadly could not raise the full amount. Eventually it was shipped to Scotland and was sold for £850. I often wonder where it is now, the Rolls I wanted so much but never got to drive. One day, I said to myself, I would get to drive one.

Our first official day of business was one to remember. We all have to start somewhere but even so, looking back now that was no way to go about beginning a new venture. We had no money to buy petrol and only one of the cars had any in, and that was only half a tank. Petrol back then was bought in gallons and it would cost about 3/11d (three shillings and eleven pence) for each one. In today's money that would be something like 20p, now the price is close to £6. We were hoping for a few customers so we could at least fill the others up.

All morning we sat there, staring at the phone. By this time the excitement of continually polishing cars had worn thin and so we opted to watch this piece of plastic on the office desk. Just as we were beginning to think about finding a new pastime something wonderful happened. The sound of ringing echoed around the office. The old fashioned ring, a trill bell sound that jolted your nerves if you were sat too close. We stared at it for a while, mostly in disbelief.

Suddenly all hell broke loose. We both made a grab for it, jostling and barging to be the first to pick it up. I can't remember who actually won and took the call, but we were just glad it wasn't the rent man! It was a real customer and we carefully went through our professional, well-rehearsed greeting ceremony. It was a well-spoken woman who wanted a car to take herself and her husband to London airport. I was down to drive first, my brain was speeding along and this was it, our first job. A nice little trip that would bring us the much-needed cash; four pounds and ten shillings to be exact. We might even be able to put petrol in the other cars now.

Then it struck us, what if this was an account customer? That would mean no payment for another month. We had enough petrol to get to the airport and make the drop, but not enough to get back, now what do we do? Panic was beginning to take hold as we prepared for the job. How would we get around this problem? On our very first job too!

If ever we needed that little bit of luck, right now was the time and thankfully we got it. The job turned out to be cash payment. I was so relieved I could have pole-vaulted to London Airport. Not much use when you have to take customers, it is not the most comfortable method of transport after all. Panic over, we finally got the start we wanted and the cars got some petrol.

After our first apprehensive weeks the business slowly began to pick up. More and more work came in and we were slowly moving into a more secure position. We could even afford to fill all of the cars up again. It was at this point my partner, who shall remain nameless, decided to make a break from the business. Nameless not because I want to protect him but simply because I can't actually remember his name! I never found out why he made the choice to leave. He moved back to Lancashire never to be heard of again.

This left me on my own after buying his share of the business and deciding to go it alone. It was another brave move, leaving me with my own full business. From postman to driver, from driver to part-owner and now from part-owner to full owner – step forward the businessman Mike Fountain.

Life was on the up and I had dreams of being the Rockefeller of Harpenden. I felt ecstatic, at least for a few minutes. Then I realised I didn't have any drivers now. I quickly needed to advertise. Turning to newspapers I placed a cunningly worded advert to the effect of 'I need some drivers'. The response I got you could very easily call disappointing; three applicants. Despite this initial setback, the business survived, the cars got petrol and my life was moving forward at a steady pace. I even made enough money to get another car. A brand new black Ford Corsair, which I had to get on special order. It had to be modified to carry extra passengers. To make the room it had a full bench seat in the front, a result of which was having the gear change moved to the steering column. The extra car and extra work meant only one thing, an extra driver. Remembering my old mate Charlie, the one who was responsible for all this in the first place, I decided to get my revenge and employ him as a full-time driver. That will teach him to stand on my foot.

Chapter 3 – Driver For Hire

Now that we had set the groundwork for the business it was just a matter of hard work and professionalism. Gradually through the next couple of years the business steadily became more popular and we grew to have a fine reputation for first-class service.

At the same time Morecambe and Wise were getting large audiences both on television and at the theatres. They were quickly becoming the household favourites but still I hadn't heard of them or taken much notice. I was more concerned with taking the business forward, not only getting the cars up to scratch but also the drivers. I decided that all drivers now needed a uniform to set us apart from the cheaper companies. Navy-blue suits and of course navy-blue hats to match, we all looked great even though underneath I think we all felt we looked like prats. The new uniforms suited all occasions from wedding to funerals and sometimes both at the same time, but it was yet another thing we had to keep clean.

Our clients came from all walks of life, wanting all kinds of driving work. Families going to the airport to fly off on holiday or meet a relative coming back from one, business men going to conferences and the previously mentioned weddings, funeral and special functions. It was during these years that Eric Morecambe first started to use our services. He would pop in from time to time and ask us to drive him and the family to various locations. More often than not Joan, his wife, would make the initial telephone call to organise times and pick up. In these early days it wasn't always myself that drove him, but I did have the pleasure of taking the family to

London and Morecambe on many occasions. The very first occasion was the 26th February 1969, it was the wedding anniversary of Eric's parents, Sadie and George and was the first time I had been to the Lancashire resort of Morecambe; the first of many that would eventually lead me to live there.

Business was improving all the time and we soon got wind that another small taxi company in the area was ripe for a merger. In a strange twist the owner was due to retire and was looking to sell up – sound familiar? Our workload was increasing and we needed the extra cars and drivers, this could be an easy solution. Merging with another local company also gave us the chance to wipe out any competition that could have sprung up had someone else jumped in before us. A brilliant business plan, even if we thought so ourselves, that could bring in even more money.

The deal went through giving us not only premises at the railway station in Harpenden, but also three more cars. Two black Morris Oxfords and a Humber Super Snipe. They also had an old London Beardmore taxi cab, which proved very popular with one particular American client who fell in love with it and bought it straight away. It was soon shipped off to America and we never saw it again.

The premises were a very simple affair by today's standards. Given the same room today would have drivers refusing to work and walking out. It was a small office with hardly any facilities and no running water. If we fancied a drink we had to go to the railway station booking office and boil the kettle. The high counter took up half of the room with wooden bench seating taking the rest. With a squeeze you could get six people in there and we were glad of the business. If it was raining though, it was more like Piccadilly than Harpenden. Bodies squashed in, all peering out into the rain, hoping not to get squeezed out into the rain by the other jostling crowd. It was just a shame they all didn't want a taxi.

Eric had continued to use us through this period of change and became one of our regulars. He got treated just like every other passenger, extremely well. We didn't use him or advertise with his name; back then things like that just didn't happen, he was just another fare. We were providing a professional service, something which later would work to my advantage.

We were now into the late 60s and quickly approaching the 70s with the wind at our backs. Life was hectic; all we seemed to do was drive and grab some sleep whenever we could. I think I did more driving than the rest of them, it certainly felt like it. The owner of the taxi firm we merged with, Bill, was a family man with a wife and kids, which meant he preferred to be at home at normal times. For me, still single, it was the early morning and late night jobs. Driving people to the airports for their flights and picking them up again a week later.

We also took over a lucrative contract with British Rail, which meant waiting outside railway stations for the last train to make sure the passengers were not stranded. It was me who did most of these too, often meaning I didn't get home until the early hours, knowing I would have to be up early again for the airport run. There I was thinking I had got away from the early shift!

Life was also getting busy for Morecambe and Wise, although I was far too shattered to even know that then. By this time they were on their sixth series for ATV and were becoming big business. Demand for them grew meaning that they too were burning the candle at both ends. A desire to provide for his family and the ever present need to keep in the public eye began to take its toll on Eric. They had already made three big films as well as their TV work, radio work, variety shows, guest appearances, summer seasons and advertisements. They wanted more though, they wanted their shows to be in colour, something ATV were only just starting to do but the BBC were already doing.

It must have played heavily on Eric's mind. Moving stations would be a huge upheaval, would it work? Would they flop or would it be their making? Looking back I can sympathise, in a smaller way, I went through similar questions in my mind. The decision was made and they finally made the switch to the BBC in June 1968, taking their writers with them. Tragically in November of the same year after only producing one series, the pressure finally became too much for his body and Eric suffered his first heart attack. Played down to the press, Joan would later reveal that it was indeed a "massive heart attack" and that he had been suffering from chest pains for quite a while.

Eric was now the property of the BBC and they took unprecedented measures to make sure he was comfortable and well looked after. He and Ernie were their investments after all, and if they were to make them money, they needed them fit and well. The BBC, despite costing them money, took the decision to temporarily get Eric a driver. Someone who could deliver him to rehearsals and recordings, wait for him and then take him back home again. Someone professional, who wouldn't abuse the position and who had a nice hat.

The BBC of course, had several car firms in London that they used for special occasions and really big stars in one-off specials. They wanted to use one of these despite it costing a fortune, after all this was Eric Morecambe. Eric however didn't seem happy to use someone he didn't know and much preferred to be driven by someone local and someone he trusted. He took the steps of getting a quote from us and taking it to the BBC for consideration, pointing out his preference in the process. This would mean a solid twelve month contract, guaranteed work and guaranteed payment for us, we kept our fingers crossed and cleaned our hats just in case.

Eventually we were told we had got it; what a feeling. If you are in business there is no greater news than knowing you have a reliable and regular payment coming in for the next twelve months. It means you can plan for the future, happy in the knowledge that the funds will be there. Everyone was happy, we had the contract, Eric got someone he knew and trusted and the BBC got a cheap deal. Unbeknown to me though, this was the time that Eric had been going through a worrying part of his recovery. With his heart attack no one knew if he would ever work again and show business people often don't hang around to find out. Their writers Sid Green and Dick Hills, tempted back to ATV with their own show, decided to leave without telling hardly anyone. This now left Morecambe and Wise without writers for the first time in eight years.

During those first few weeks he never talked about his health. Some days he would be better than others, that was obvious, but he just got on with his job. He knew his limitations and worked around them for the first few shows. No one knew watching the end result just how ill he was; that is testament to his work ethic and professionalism.

He eventually recovered enough to begin a second series and the BBC managed to find Eric and Ernie a new writer in the form of Ken Dodd's gagman, Eddie Braben. Initially Eric, Ernie and Eddie didn't believe the partnership would work. Eddie's writing style did not suit how the boys worked; they didn't do quick-fire one-liners, they preferred crosstalk and short sketches. Luckily, the head of entertainment at the BBC, Bill Cotton, saw things differently. He got them together in his office and sat back while Eddie observed them and Eric and Ernie discussed possible ideas.

The end result was that Eddie would write five episodes and see how things went. There were anxieties all round about this, but Eric being Eric, treated it as a challenge as I'm sure did Eddie himself. Whatever he produced would be a departure from the Sid and Dick typical double act routines, and these were apprehensive times. Eric and Ernie were perfectionists and no doubt gave their new writer a run for his money, in return Eddie changed the dynamic of the act giving both Eric and Ernie something to work with and improve. Eric became less gormless but still childlike while Ernie got his own character; the pompous writer. In essence Eddie wrote for the real people, he brought out what he had seen in that meeting and in doing so created something that would endear viewers to them. In the end, Eric was pleased at the outcome and the way the act had made the transition to stronger, more rounded characters.

The rehearsals for the show started and I drove Eric to the rooms at Dalgarno Way in London. The room was part of a community centre in the middle of a rundown council estate close to Wormwood Scrubs. Eric liked it there, it was out of the way and he felt they could be left alone to concentrate on this new series. My opinion of Eric changed during these first few months; my apprehension at working for such an exulted star was completely washed away. I don't know really what I expecting but he certainly wasn't what people might consider a high-flying star. He wasn't pompous or evasive, he didn't think he was better than you; he was a normal, down-to-earth person. The only way he differed from everyone else was his humour. He had a lightning-quick wit and it took me a while to actually get up to his speed of thinking.

I dropped him off and made my way back to the TV centre to have lunch with the security team there while they pounded the boards and refined the script. This was the first show after his heart attack and the public would be watching. There was certainly more pressure than usual on him, but as ever, he worked through it. That first show of that series featured Peter Cushing, the star of the Hammer horror films. He was a big name back then, a real star. Having met him, I, like Eric and Ernie, found him to be the most gentle and kind person. Quite opposite from his film persona, and a real surprise.

As the first show began actual recording, I was there with Joan and his children, Gail and Gary. The audience were nervous, the crew were nervous, Eddie Braben had to leave the studio, it was so tense. The music started and everyone took a deep breath and waited. Eric and Ernie walked on to welcoming but reserved applause. No one knew what would happen, Eric must have been worried but the first line, the single most important line probably he ever delivered completely changed the atmosphere.

Eric, glanced down at his chest, patted it gently and said; "Keep going you fool." It was a throwback to the variety days and was a gag often used back then, but on this day, on this show, with this man it was something altogether different. The whole room breathed a single huge sigh of relief, the tension had gone and the show could start. Joan smiled, she knew he was back, she knew the tension had suddenly evaporated and all the fears and worries had gone. Eddie heard the laughs and came back in to join us, he too was smiling, Eric and Ernie began to enjoy themselves and relax; the new material was working, and how! It was a hugely successful return to television and to form for them both.

With the show complete I collected Eric and his family to take them home. For him the nerves didn't stop at that point. Everyone else was so relieved and so excited that Morecambe and Wise were back, but not Eric. This was just the recording, it had to be broadcast yet, the public had the final say, and he was genuinely worried about what they would think. Whenever I collected him after a performance he would always ask me how I thought it went. It was different being an observer and easier to gauge than actually being in the middle of it.

We all know now that it was a huge success, the building block for the rest of their careers, but for Eric, it was just another worry. How would the public react? Were the audience just being nice? Would the new writing style work? Would his health keep up? Would the new characters created by Eddie be too different from what the public expected? So many things, all at the same time and so very close to his heart attack. How he managed I'll never know, but once that first line hit home, you were in his world. A world he loved and wanted everyone to be a part of. A world he and Ernie would remain at the top of for the next 14 years, a world where they are still loved to this very day.

They were just starting on their new journey, a whole series to look forward to and more to come. For me I knew that soon my contract would end and I would be back actively looking for more clients to fill the void. No one could ever take Eric's place, but I needed to survive, just like Eric had done. Where would the next job come from?

Chapter 4 – New Start

With the BBC contract in its final few weeks we were not actively looking for any extra work from them or Eric. We were a business and these things happen. Contracts come and go and you just get on with it. It was nice to know Eric had recovered and that the shows would go on, but business is business.

In the dying days of the contract Eric came in to see us. He was cheerful and looking healthy and we assumed it was just to say thank you and goodbye. This however, was not the case. What he had come to say would be the pivotal point in my life, and in a few short moments he would ask me a single question that would turn my life upside down.

"Would you like to come and work full-time for me Michael?" he said smiling. I guess he knew the implications it would have and thinking back it was a great privilege to have even been considered let alone be asked.

By this time our business had grown again, taking over a third company giving us more cars and drivers. The merger with Bill meant that he was still part-owner, which threw even more questions into the mix. The only thing that kept spinning around in my head was what I would say when people asked me what I did for a living.

"And what do you do?"

"I am Eric Morecambe's chauffeur."

I liked the sound of that, but it still worried me. All these things flying around my head, barging to the fore and demanding answers I just didn't have. In a split second there must have been dozens and more queuing up waiting to surprise me. It seemed like there was a competition in my head to see which question could surprise or scare me the most. It would mean giving up the business and that would be hard. It would also mean giving up the long hours, late nights, early mornings and the cramped office on rainy days. That would not be so hard. It would mean leaving my friends, the other drivers and Charlie. It would mean handing over the company I had struggled to build over the last five years. I had taken it from part-time driving, through full-time driving, part-ownership and full ownership. Taken the leap and merged with another company, strived to keep the standards high and produced a successful and viable business. Could I just leave all that behind and start out again from scratch?

You bet.

It took me all of two seconds to answer Eric's question and the rest of the day to worry about it. It would change my life forever. My head was full of even more questions after I had agreed, most of which still didn't have answers. The kind of questions that stop people from stepping forward and taking on their future face-to-face. Would it work out? Would I fail? Would I have to go back to my normal job? Would I get on with Eric now that he is paying? How would my life change? Would Eric change? Could I just leave the business I had built up from almost nothing?

This was not only a new start for Eric, but for me as well. I had decided to leave the things that I had worked for, the things I knew, and I was moving into a brand new and exciting world. It wasn't an unknown for me; I had driven Eric many times before, but not as his personally paid chauffeur.

I made an agreement with the co-owner that suited us both and I left him with the company minus one of the cars. Even a professional chauffeur needs his own wheels.

As the first day approached, nervous was not a word that could adequately convey how I felt. Petrified may be too strong, but certainly somewhere in-between. I didn't have to worry though, Eric soon made me feel at home, and he had that gift with anyone he met. He could instantly put you at ease and make you feel like you've known him all your life. That is a wonderful talent that so few people have.

A question I am always asked is, "What was Eric like?" Wherever I go, whoever I speak to, they want to know what he was like in real life. They feel a bond with him and want to be reassured that he wasn't a fake and that he really was that funny all of the time.

He was a star, but a star with his feet planted firmly on the ground. Very down to earth, very intelligent and a great talker. He would go out of his way to please people whether they were the director of a television network or a stranger in the street. To Eric they were his audience and he had to leave them laughing, and he always did. It didn't matter how he was feeling, it wasn't about him. He was compelled to make people happy, it was his duty and I think his destiny to entertain. He had been given this wonderful thing and he would use is at every opportunity, sometimes despite feeling very ill himself.

For Eric, the first meeting he had with people was very important to him; first impressions were everything. He had to put you at ease; he had to make you feel you knew him because after he had succeeded in that, you were captivated. You were his audience and he could weave his magic on you without you even knowing or being aware how hard he was trying. That was why he went off like a steam train, his brain going full speed, pulling out the appropriate gags for the situation. If one fell short, the next was following it on until he got you to laugh, then he could ease up a little, he had you.

Over the years I began to realise that this initial burst of energy he had was in fact his way of dealing with nerves. Yes, Eric Morecambe was nervous about meeting new people, probably more than you would realise. The person stood in front of him, meeting their hero for the first time must have been very scared, but unbeknown to them, hiding behind a constant flow of jokes and patter was an equally scared entertainer. I have often asked myself why? Why would a man seemingly full of confidence, who could make you laugh by simply walking into a room, be scared? The answer is simple; because he was just like the rest of us. Just because he was an entertainer and television personality didn't make him immune to anxiety.

Eric was a normal person that just happened to have a very remarkable talent. That didn't stop him from having the same feelings and emotions as everyone else. His great skill was to take you into his world without you knowing it. Having you laughing so hard that you were unable to draw breath, even to speak to him. Then you were in his domain and he was king.

He was also a gentleman, a real gentleman, something sadly not seen very often these days. He didn't swear in front of ladies (or at all really), he opened doors for people, he thought of others before himself, just a genuinely nice person, He didn't want to be 'the star', for him that concept didn't exist. He hated that side of the business. What you saw with Eric is what you got, the genuine article.

He often joked in the car during our journeys. It took me time, but eventually I grew accustomed to the tremendous speed his brain could operate at and his style of humour. You could sometimes see a tag line coming but it never lessened the effect. You would often hear the same joke over and over again as he pulled it from a bottomless pit of gags at the many functions he attended. With Eric though, it never got less funny. He had this presence, this enthusiasm for the laugh, he put his all into every joke and it made a huge difference.

This talent had seen him through the bad times, the short runs, the dismal reviews and ill health. It gave him the trappings of a star but he would never be so crass as to brag. Amongst these were his house in Harpenden, his close friends, his family of course and his personal favourite at the time, a car, the Jensen Interceptor.

Although some of the cars at the hire company were good, this was a serious step up in class now, which only got better as time went on and the arrival of the first Rolls Royce.

I have driven, crashed and fallen off many things in my past, but the Rolls must be the pinnacle. With the amount of accidents I had, it's surprising I even considered chauffeuring as a career.

My first form of transport, and I use that word in its widest terms, was a small Piatti 125cc scooter that won no prizes for looks or performance. I spent most of the time not actually riding it but picking it up after falling off. It didn't take much to unsettle the little thing; a sudden gust of wind through an open gate often did the trick. There you would be, happily riding through the countryside, past fields, fences and hedges on each side of the road and then suddenly there would be a gate. As you passed there was nothing to hold back the wind and even a slight gust would give you something to think about. One minute riding along and the next thing you knew you would be thrown sideways, blown completely off of the bike. The Piatti also didn't like corners very much, especially when there was even a hint of frost. Quite often you would turn into a corner only to discover the scooter ignored the wheels and carried straight on. You on the other hand, very often didn't.

Lesson learnt, I moved on to the Vespa, a much more solid scooter and less prone to throwing you off at every opportunity. Having managed not to break it or myself, I scraped together enough money to buy a Lambretta. This 175cc scooter was all the rage in the early 60s along with Cliff Richard, Craig Douglas, Eden Kane and coffee shops with jukeboxes.

Scooters are all well and good, but a real pain to ride, literally sometimes, when the weather is anything but sunny. Riding from Harpenden to Hoddesdon seemed only a few inches on the map but by the time I got there I was like a snowman. My black motorcycle suit was completely white and I had lost all feeling in my fingers and toes. A shot of hot coffee whilst listening to "Only Sixteen" by Sam Cooke in a coffee bar soon sorted me out though, but there was always the return journey to look forward to.

Sticking with two wheels, I briefly had a BSA 125 that wasn't involved in any wind related accidents. It was never stopped by the police, had breakdowns or catapulted me into a field. Maybe the reason for lack of accidents was because I didn't have it very long before I finally saw the light and traded it in for a car. More about my car history later, but for now back to the Jensen.

This powerful V8, 3-speed automatic sports car was a truly wonderful thing. It had the looks of an Aston Martin, plush leather interior, wooden dashboard, curved rear window, a real driver's car. The automatic gearbox had a kick-down accelerator that really whipped your head back, pure excitement that hugged the road and was a joy to drive. It was marketed as a two-seater plus, the plus being a tiny bench seat it the back that was a struggle to get to. It was a two-seater sports car, simple as that, despite what the adverts said.

That was its only problem. It couldn't really be used as a chauffeur driven vehicle if Eric and Joan wanted to go out together. Someone had to be screwed up in the back and it invariably was Eric. It was the car however, I used to ferry him to and from rehearsals, and with more new series rapidly approaching, the hard work was about to start, and the need for something more comfortable grew. Soon I would fulfil my dream of actually driving a Rolls Royce.

Chapter 5 – Rolling Along

The car most associated with Eric Morecambe, and in fact any top celebrity at the time, was a Rolls Royce. That was the car that made people stop in the street, watching in awe as it glided past, straining to catch a glimpse of the owner whilst completely ignoring the driver. If the car also had a personalised number plate, this caused even more excitement, the owner must really be famous, not to mention rich.

EM 100 was the number plate in question and it was attached to a metallic brown Rolls Royce, now synonymous with Eric. This wasn't Eric's first Rolls though, his first one was a Mk1 Silver Shadow that was aptly painted silver, or more accurately, 'Shell Grey'.

Morecambe and Wise were big names with a hugely successful, long-running series for ATV. Having just made the jump to the BBC and topping the polls, it is a mystery as to why he went for it in the first place. Looking back, both neither he nor I actually liked the colour but nevertheless, that was his and my very first Rolls Royce.

A Rolls Royce was a big leap from the cars of my youth, that to be honest, probably mirrored most adolescent boys then and now. Amongst the first was a green Triumph Herald that had a distinctly special safety feature. Applying full lock to turn around caused the engine to stall, often leaving you powerless in the middle of a road. This was followed by an Austin Mini, Austin 1800, Sunbeam Alpine and a Morris van that I painted black to try, unsuccessfully, to hide the GPO signage.

As each car collapsed in a mass of radiator steam and broken cogs more followed. A bright yellow Toyota bought for the single reason my daughter liked the colour and a Daimler Lanchester I got for £85. Next came a Renault convertible that had strength issues; any weight in the back such as passengers caused the whole thing to sag, stopping the doors from closing. As that car died a Ford Anglia replaced it; green with a white roof similar to one in Heartbeat. Moving on and next for the Mike Fountain scrapyard was an Austin Maestro, which sadly had to be sold, mainly because the wheels kept falling off. It's no wonder someone introduced the M.O.T. test!

Stepping from my list of broken and discarded wrecks into a Rolls was like moving into another world. They are truly wonderful cars; sheer luxury. Leather interior with polished walnut dashboard and an engine that sounded like a cat purring, that is if you can get a 6.8 litre cat! At no point did the wheels fall off, it never sagged and unlike some of my previous cars, it never retained three inches of water in the footwells when it rained.

As we approached 1974, the Morecambe and Wise shows were massive, absolutely huge. This of course meant they were in demand a lot more, which in turn meant they were earning more. It was probably this fact that finally nudged Eric to consider, at long last, getting rid of the Rolls. The realisation must have been slowly creeping up on him that this first car wasn't really for him. If anything, the colour didn't sit right, but there was something else that you just couldn't put your finger on. You know when something isn't quite right, and we both had that feeling about that particular Silver Shadow.

Around the same time and perhaps because of his decision to sell the first Rolls, he also thought it might be a good idea to look into getting a personalised number plate. He had always fancied one and now would be the ideal time, but first he needed a car to put it on. After a good deal of searching he finally settled on a brand new one. Still the same make and model, but this time the one most recognised as his car, the metallic walnut Silver Shadow Mk1. There were a few new features like more advanced steering and wider wheels which improved roadholding no end, and the icing on the cake, his own private plate, EM 100.

The car came from Jack Barclay of London in October 1974, and they were also charged with finding an appropriate number plate. In those days there was no Internet, and looking for something like that was no easy task. One was located and finally tracked down to an old Austin. With the paperwork completed and much to Eric's delight, it was finally added to the car.

It was a wonderful vehicle to drive. Elegant, smooth, great to handle and a pleasure to clean – most of the time. People forget just how much hard work goes into keeping a car like that in pristine condition, and I was the man responsible for it. You can't have a Rolls Royce Silver Shadow with a personalised number plate and turn up at an event with mud and dead insects all over it. The times I have washed and cleaned that car, polished it, fuelled it, on the odd occasion fixed it. It was almost like part of the family. You do grow fond of something you spend nearly all your time with, and it was a sad day when we parted company.

The car is still on the road, or rather garaged somewhere. Joan Morecambe put it up for sale in 2005 and it was bought on December 4th at auction by three businessmen for around £36,000. I think the plan was to hire it out or use it for weddings, but I have only seen it a few times since then. It was sold complete with Eric's eight-track system and collection of music tapes, including Shirley Bassey and Frank Zappa.

Back to the 1970s and what I used to call, "The Mike Fountain Get The Car Ready Today Programme".

If the car was going to be needed a particular day I would start early. Out came the hosepipe, leathers, polish, dusters and no end of things that made it shine and glint in the sun. It was a large car and it wasn't a quick job. You just can't rush something like that. You had to be gentle and treat it with respect. Remove every last speck of dirt, streaky lines or smudges and then out with the bees Turtle Wax.

Extra attention had to be lavished on the chrome parts like the huge front grill and of course the Flying Lady mascot.

That mascot was not easy to clean. So many small places for the wax to get into, and you just couldn't leave it there. Painstakingly I had to polish every curve and contour, but in the end it was worth it. I knew that Eric would never walk round and inspect the car, he wasn't that kind of person, but he did expect it to be perfect; and he expected perfection from me.

I have only mentioned the outside so far, but the same care and attention was given to the interior as well, if anything more so, because that's the part that people see close up. The walnut dashboard had to be cleaned and polished, the leather seats, the door handles, everything. You couldn't expect a guest to climb in and have to move old magazines out of the way, or have them reach for the door handle only to discover it was dirty and covered in chocolate from the kids. The boot could be filled with any old junk, fishing tackle, props, shoes, but that never got seen. It was the interior that people would judge you on and it was my job to make sure it was perfect. Yes it was a hard life being the chauffeur – but I wouldn't have changed it for the world.

Once it was all complete and the sun was shining it made you feel really proud, especially if you were going to be driving it. That's the best part and it makes all the work worthwhile. If you had a Rolls Royce back then, people would say that you've made it. Eric, at one time, had two; what does that say I wonder? He didn't have two as any kind of status symbol; it was just the period between the two cars when he had the grey-silver one and the new metallic brown one. Some photographs exist of them both together, I took a few, but alas they have long since been lost.

I am not sure if it was Eric's comic side, but the one thing that he really wanted having now got his new Rolls, was to have his initials, in gold lettering, on the doors. Not content with having a brand new Silver Shadow and a personal number plate, he wanted to go that extra step. I duly set about the task, and managed to get his initials on the doors. He was over the moon with the end result, and using only small letters, approximately one inch high, the EM on each door didn't look too tacky. They remained there for quite some time, only fading after several years so that they were only visible if you looked very, very closely, or you were the one who put them there!

Just going back to the Flying Lady; he also had two of those, on the same car. The original one was stolen and it was the only time I have ever seen Eric be what can only be best described as angry.

The car was parked up outside the Guildhall in Preston and I had gone inside to get Eric. He and Ernie were doing one of their whistle-stop shows that they fondly called bank raids. They would rush to the theatre, do the show and rush back home a few thousand pounds better off. The bank raids were fun and covered most areas of the UK. We shall learn more of these escapades later on, but for now, the continued story of the Flying Lady.

As we walked towards the car it soon became evident that she had gone. Eric and Ernie were known not to use bad language, but on that day I can tell you, the words that came out of Eric's mouth would shock many people. The car he had always wanted, the car he loved, the car he had worked hard for, had been vandalised.

I too was angry; it was like someone had broken my own car. What is astonishing is how they actually got it off. The Rolls Royce lady is a solid piece of silver fixed to the car; it doesn't move, it doesn't have screws, it's part of the car.

That incident really upset him for a while afterwards, even though he got a new one. I think it was the reasoning rather than the actual act. Who on earth would steal a thing like that and why? What possible value could it be? You can't sell it to another Rolls Royce owner; they have enough money to buy any number of them. You can't sell it openly, or even talk about it in public. Somewhere in Preston, someone has a useless bit of metal that says only one thing – they are a thief. Not exactly something to be proud of.

The lady wasn't the only thing to come off the car though, and despite their reputation, on occasions other objects have become unattached. I must say at this point, these things happen very rarely though, but they do happen. Driving one for over twenty years I have known various bits suddenly disappearing, and not due to thieves.

The problem is, if something falls off a Rolls, you can't just leave it; it probably costs a lot of money. This is why, on one occasion, Eric had to stop and get out. Not usually a problem, but this day it was raining heavily, and the bit that fell off was the windscreen wiper. We couldn't stop straight away, it wasn't safe, so we had to travel a few yards further, straining to see the road through the rapidly blurring windscreen. Finally I managed to find a safe spot and pulled over. Eric looked at me.

"Well, someone's got to get it," he said, looking me up and down.

Luckily he wasn't the type of person who ordered people about and he didn't mind getting a bit wet, so he quickly opened the door and vanished into the rain. A short while later he emerged from the rain and clambered back into the car victoriously clutching the aforementioned part. He didn't mind getting a bit wet, but when he got back in he was absolutely soaked. I must admit to stifling a laugh, seeing Eric sat there, absolutely drenched, nursing a broken windscreen wiper and glancing at me as if to say; "Not a word... don't you say a word!"

My mirth was to be repaid sometime later. Different road, same car, same weather, same wiper, same result. The one main difference was that this time it was me who got the soaking. One all. It wasn't all laughter and car polish!

Driving though was the most enjoyable part of the job for me. It is where you see and hear things, catch snippets of conversation or even join in. You meet famous people, even royalty, and there is much to tell about the many passengers. If only the car could tell its own story but sadly it can't. Luckily I can.

Chapter 6 – In The Back

Of all the celebrities to appear on the Morecambe and Wise show, very few needed persuading. It seemed that the more famous they were, the more they wanted to be on the show. They didn't mind what would happen because they knew they would be treated with utmost respect. At the same time they would become Eric and Ern's stooge, and even possibly appear in one of Ernie's infamous plays. They knew they would not be talked down to or made to look stupid. They would not be insulted or treated like idiots, something modern programme makers should take note of.

As Eric and Ern's popularity grew, from the early 1970s onwards, being asked to appear along with them was seen as a great honour, even more so if it was their long anticipated Christmas shows. Famously, Glenda Jackson was spotted playing Cleopatra in the famous sketch, and as a result was asked to appear in the film *A Touch Of Class*, for which she won an Oscar. Eric and Ernie sent her a telegram saying, "Stick with us kid and we'll get you another one!"

It wasn't the awards or accolades that drew the stars; it was the chance to say that they had appeared with Morecambe and Wise, and that they had great fun in doing so.

The producer of the shows from 1968 to 1974, and later after they had moved to Thames, was John Ammonds. A vastly experienced man who helped bring out the laughter and really understood what they, along with Eddie Braben, the scriptwriter, were trying to achieve. He knew how to use the cameras to get the best out of a gag, he knew when to move in for a close up and he knew when to just leave the boys alone and let their personality do all the work.

It was John who sourced the guest stars, approached the agents and fought off requests from people desperate to get on stage with the boys. Many of the stars simply agreed without even knowing what they were going to do, so high was their desire to work on the programme.

Despite people queuing up to appear with them, one of the few who had second thoughts was a young actress called Sarah Miles. Unbeknown to John, she was reticent to appear, and so the usual course of persuasive tactics was put into action. Plan one, which usually worked, was to take the star and their agent for a nice meal to discuss matters. After actually meeting Eric and Ern over lunch, no one could refuse, could they?

Eric, Ernie, John, Sarah and her agent were duly driven to an expensive restaurant in London with the idea that Eric and Ern would charm her into appearing. She was nervous for some reason but Eric was confident he could easily persuade her, and that things would be just fine. The meal went down very well. Eric and Ernie turned on the charm and just to make sure they were forever refilling her glass with wine. At the end of the meal and much to Eric's surprise, the plan did not work and she still wouldn't agree on the appearance. They all climbed into the Rolls and we were now forced to use the rarely used plan B.

Plan B was a subterfuge; starting with an offer to return the people to the TV Centre. They had to say yes of course, or be left stranded at the restaurant. Under this pretence, and already plied with wine, we took a different, alternative route back; a route that just happened to pass several pubs.

"Oh, I've not been in there for a while. Let's just pop in for a quick one Michael." Eric would say.

As each pub was left behind and more alcohol had been consumed, the atmosphere in the car slowly changed from businesslike, through happy, and was now firmly at hilarious. Eric and Ernie were in full flow much to the delight of the other passengers. Bits of their act were thrown in, old crosstalk routines, ad-libbing at things in the street, the full-on Eric and Ernie experience. By the time we got back to the studios having visited at least five pubs, she had agreed to everything; it was almost like one of Ern's plays. Everyone was pleased at a job well done, even if they had to go further than usual and use the unusual approach of plan B.

Their delight didn't last for long though. I guess the alcohol wore off after a while. A few days later she called John and cancelled everything she had agreed previously. Eric told me it was out of pure fear, and that she didn't want to "ruin her reputation as a serious actress". I expect that she was kicking herself later when greats such as Dame Flora Robson and Frank Finlay appeared on the show. None of whom, it must be pointed out, had their reputations tarnished. If anything, they were loved more for being a good sport, and their fans saw a whole new side to them.

Another well-known person who didn't appear and who also took a ride in the Rolls was one of Eric's comedy heroes; Arthur Askey. Eric idolised him from a very early age and always thought he had one of the sharpest wits in show business. He often said he wanted to be like him at his age; sadly he never made that age, but in my opinion he surpassed him in comic skills. Arthur was one of the very rare few who actually upstaged Eric at a public function. Just think about that for a second. Eric, the man with a thousand one-liners and a gag for every occasion getting upstaged by Arthur Askey.

It happened at a social event they were both attending to celebrate Arthur's 50 years in show business held by the Variety Club of Great Britain. Arthur being the resident entertainer, like all good comics he always felt the need to make people laugh. He reached up, grabbed his glasses and shook them, mimicking Eric's famous gag.

"I don't know where you got the idea of wearing big glasses and being funny for a living." He said in a loud voice, much to the delight of the audience.

Eric was stuck for an instant reply. Luckily people were still howling at Arthur's quip, giving him a few minutes to work out how to come back without offending his idol. Eventually though his usually razor-quick mind kicked in and he leant forward. The guests look on and quietened down.

"Oh sit down Dad!"

It was a great retort, even if it was a bit late. But of all the people Eric wouldn't mind being upstaged by, Arthur was surely top of the pile, if not the only person on the list.

I found Arthur a surprisingly down-to-earth ordinary man in his twilight years. He had rather a rough ride towards the end and was very ill in hospital. Eric had visited him several times before he died. Arthur was really pleased that Eric had taken the time to see him, but when the end came, it hit Eric even more. When someone you idolise passes away, the well-used adage is true and I knew a little part of Eric died that day. Eric took his own time to recover privately but in public he was his usual charming and funny self. I knew deep down though he was running on automatic for a few weeks.

It was not only television celebrities and family that graced the back seat of the Rolls.

It started out as a normal evening and I was to drive Eric and Joan to The Grosvenor Hotel for a night of fundraising on behalf of the Lord's Taverners. Eric was the president at that time, 1978, and always did his best to help them raise money. As we rolled into the Park Lane entrance we were met by the secretary of the society who had a strange request. Would it be possible for me to pick up the guest of honour at short notice?

"What do you mean by short notice?" Eric asked.

"Now."

Eric agreed and I was told to make my way to Kensington Palace and collect the Duke and Duchess of Kent. Upon hearing this I was cast back to my first days of driving for Eric. The excitement, the eagerness to do a good job, the awful rumbling in my stomach! Doesn't that mean… isn't that… I mean… my head was spinning as Eric discussed the finer details with the secretary. It was not planned so I suppose there was no time for nerves to fully kick in, or thinking about how to behave in front of them, it was just one of those strange moments that tend to happen when you least expect it. One minute you're driving Eric Morecambe, next a member of the royal family jumps in!

The situation hit me as I turned the car around and headed in the direction of the palace. I was on my way now, alone with my thoughts. I would be responsible for the safe arrival of royalty, me, an ex-postman, ex-taxi driver and bad gardener from Harpenden. My earlier driving days came in handy and the professional in me took over. I got there in what seemed like no time at all and slowly passed through the police security at the gates. I suppose they didn't think twice about a Rolls Royce arriving with a rather shaky man behind the wheel.

Like so many other well-known people I have met during my career, they were really nice and put me at ease quickly. You don't think about these things but even royalty are people. They have the same thoughts, hopes and fears, and the same interest in Eric Morecambe. They must have known who I was because as soon as they climbed in, they started asking me about Eric. What was he like? Was he always that funny? The exact same questions asked by fans the country over. I had to smile to myself though; there I was being asked questions about Eric Morecambe by the Duke and Duchess of Kent – how far I had come!

Of the places I have visited you would have thought that Kensington Palace would have been the most difficult to get into, but it wasn't; that honour would have to be the BBC Television Centre.

On the beach with Mum and Dad

The famous Lambretta

Eric and Ernie at the Leeds Empire in 1952 with Phyllis Dixey

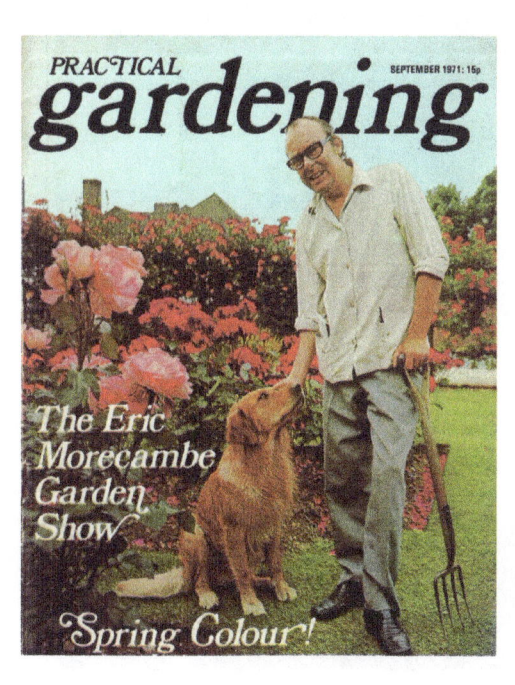

Taking credit for my work!

My wedding day

A picnic with the Karlins, an all-girl group from the 60s and 70s (me far right)
If you look very closely, you can see Eric's initials on the door

Enjoying a day at a Lord's Taverners charity cricket match

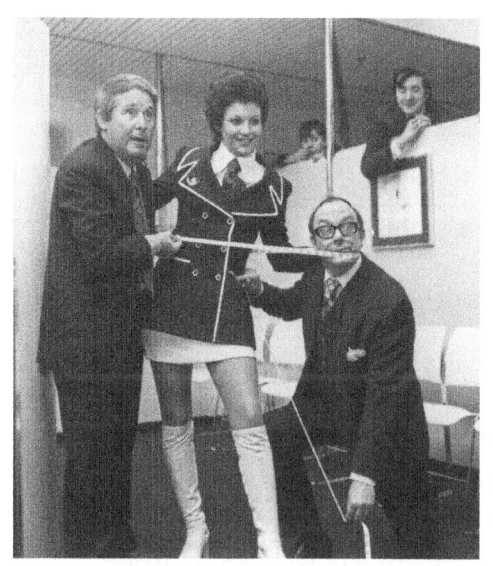

Eric and Ernie at a publicity event mid 70s

At an ATV party with Noele Gordon

Chapter 7 – The BBC

The BBC is known world over for their innovative programmes, non-biased news coverage and many, many more things. What it isn't known for though, is its ease of entry. The whole place was warm and friendly once you got in, but getting in past those barriers was the challenge. There were two barriers, one marked 'In', and the other 'Out'. Not many people got to see that second barrier because they never actually managed to get in in the first place. Alongside the barriers was a small hut, the resident of which was The Commissionaire. A word that would send shivers down the spine of any driver, and usually any passengers as well.

The Commissionaire at the BBC during the 1970s was famous. He had a strange grim determination; you wouldn't get in. As you approached he would emerge from his little hut and wait for you with a smile; you wouldn't get in. Famous name, rich, American star, latest singing sensation; still wouldn't let you in.

"If you're not on the list," he would say, "you can't come in."

He would helpfully inform you of the nearest car park, half a mile down the road, or suggest using the tube; he was nice like that. But it wasn't for this, shall we say character that he became most famous, it was because of an anecdote often told by Eric.

The man, The Commissionaire, the grimly determined gate guard was called Vic, or as Eric called him, the One-Armed Bandit. Vic had lost an arm during military action and on seeing Eric being driven up to the gates tried his luck by asking for free tickets for the show.

"Hello Mr. Morecambe. Nice to see you. You… er… don't happen to have any… er… spare tickets going do you? Always loved your shows."

Eric looked him up and down, "Sorry, but no." He said.

Vic looked upset and enquired why.

"Because," came the reply, "you can't clap."

I think he got tickets anyway, and was not hurt by the joke, in fact as I recall, he was in hysterics about it.

Eventually he got used to seeing us drive up, and because Eric always bought him a Christmas present, he would allow us in. The same can't be said for others who tried though. During some of the shows, while they were being prepared or recorded, I often visited Vic by the barrier. You may call it sadistic, but it was fun to see the celebrities told they could not come in. The look on their faces when, after perusing his list, he informed them that they were definitely not on it and they would have to park across the street.

That place holds so many happy memories for me and I was very lucky and privileged to be part of it. I enjoyed watching the shows being put together. The basic script by Eddie Braben was read and reread. Scribbles and notes were added during rehearsal as they fine-tuned it. Ad-libs were flung about and hastily added to the show and laughter filled the room. It was wonderful to witness all the small ideas and jokes come together in such a magical way, and to see all those involved participate in the creation of something that is still funny today.

Many people thought Eric ad-libbed a lot of the work, but this was only half true. If during a rehearsal he threw in an ad-lib, which he did a lot, and the rest of the team thought it was good, it was added to the script. Thereafter it was rehearsed and tweaked, practiced and honed until it looked like an ad-lib. This freedom to invent and add new ideas was nurtured by the team of Eddie Braben and the producer John Ammonds. John knew it was the only way to get the best out of someone and he was so enthusiastic that it rubbed off on all the others. Someone with as much creativity as Eric cannot be muted or the true essence of the man is lost.

Everyone in the team had a part to play no matter who they were. Lighting, sets, props, cameramen, all of them put a little extra into their job because it was Eric and Ernie, and because they felt part of something special. Some of the sets they used were just breathtaking for the time. Entertainment shows didn't do that sort of thing in the seventies; they were lucky to have a curtain and microphone sometimes. Eric and Ernie though had vision. John Ammonds and later Ernest Maxim, shared that vision and because they were who they were, things got done.

Ernest Maxim was the main dance man of the show. Even when John Ammonds was producing, he would get Ernest in for the big dance numbers. Later, when John decided to move on it was Ernest who took over the producer role, but still slotted in the magnificent MGM-style dance routines like Singing in the Rain. I remember the huge set for that routine. It was remarkable. An almost replica set of the original film with added bits for the funny sections. It took over two weeks to build it, two days to rehearse and only six minutes of screen time.

I don't think many people were looking at the set when the routine started though. All eyes were on Ernie, dancing with his umbrella. Then Eric appeared and the routine was taken to another level. The moment Ernie throws the umbrella up and misses the catch was not meant to happen. In the original script he should have caught it, but kept missing it. It was decided to kept it in as it added yet another laugh.

Eric caught a cold from all that water, but it was a small price to pay for something that will last forever. The routine was shown to Gene Kelly and he liked it so much that he had the clip prepared for him so he could take it back to America. He thought it was the best parody of his routine that had ever been made. Praise enough I think.

Any show of this calibre was hard work, and that hard work usually began with the rehearsals after Eddie's mammoth task of producing the script.

When they first began at the BBC, as mentioned before, they would rehearse in a community centre in Dalgarno Way, West London. It was quiet there and nothing disturbed them. The only time they got interrupted was when the BBC was filming a documentary about how a Morecambe and Wise show was put together. It was part of the Omnibus series called *Fools Rush In*. For any fan this is a great look behind the scenes at what really happens to create something as special as the Morecambe and Wise show. The show also featured one of my rare appearances on television, but more of that later.

The rehearsal rooms themselves were very sparse, as can be seen from the documentary, but Eric said, on many occasions, that this helped because there was nothing to distract them. No paintings, cupboards or ornaments. Just a table, some chairs and occasionally a piano. There was one telephone for the whole building that could only be used in an emergency; remember there were no mobile phones back then. There was one kettle and you had to make your own tea – even Eric and Ernie had to brew up themselves. No expense was spared… well, just no expense at all really.

The BBC spent its money elsewhere and in the day it was doing a fantastic job attracting the big names from around the world. It was the hub of all things television back then and I got to see and mix with some of the great stars. Strangely, they all wanted to know about Eric and Ernie – they were icons even to other celebrities. I suppose that was their reward for all that early grafting and hard slog.

A popular early evening programme around the 1970s was *Nationwide*. It was a kind of magazine programme covering news, local issues and the bizarre dog-ate-my-fish-tank type of stories. It went out about 6pm and on one particular day Eric and Ernie were guests. We arrived and were shown into the green room. For anyone not familiar with a television studio or television programme, there is usually a small room set up with comfortable chairs, food, drink and sometimes a television monitor showing what is being broadcast at that time. Into this room are ushered any special guests so they can relax before their appearance, and tuck into free food.

On the episode with Eric and Ernie there was also a female singing group called The Nolans. People of a certain age will instantly know them, but for those of us who are slightly younger, they were the seventies version of the Spice Girls. These girls never stopped talking. Even when Eric and Ernie were called to the studio, they constantly asked questions about them, I was glad to get out of there, a shame really as the food was really nice and probably brought in especially for Morecambe and Wise. They did these one-off appearances usually for charity or just to keep their profiles in the public eye during rehearsals, when their shows were off the screen.

As time went on the rehearsal rooms were moved to a more modern building with a purpose-built studio in Acton, North London. This place could house several shows all rehearsing at the same time and even had its own props department. Because so many different shows could be rehearsed there, I got to mingle with even more of the stars.

I bumped into Dana one day; I know it sounds like the start of an Eddie Braben joke but this is a true story. She was waiting for her car to pick her up and we got chatting. Once she found out who I was, it was the usual story; questions, questions, questions. She thought it must be a wonderful job, and she was right. There I was, sat in a Rolls Royce chatting to Dana about Eric Morecambe. What I failed to tell her, call it vanity if you want, was that I was also the gardener, cleaner and pool man – no point in ruining the image. Maybe one day she will read about it in this book and remember those days.

Strange isn't it, everyone I have ever met always thinks that being a driver for someone famous must be exciting and glamorous. They are of course mostly right, but there were times when things did not always go to plan.

Chapter 8 – The Bank Raids

Eric always called their live shows Bank Raids. Not the summer seasons or the two-month runs, but one-night shows scattered around the UK. He called them this because to him it was the same kind of approach and outcome. One day you would set off somewhere, get to the theatre, do the act and drive home as quickly as possible. There was no real rehearsals as such, the material was pretty much the same every show, give or take the odd ad-lib. The props, lighting and music was the same, so there was very little effort involved if you discount the travel. The end result was a large sum of money for standing on a stage and making people laugh.

If you were naturally funny, like Eric, then this was money for old rope. Not that they didn't enjoy it though, it was their bread and butter. Playing a live audience was something they had done from the very beginning and continued to do to the very end. It was something they always went back to when things weren't going well, knowing that their skill in working with a real audience would always bring them acclaim.

Working live is totally different from radio or television. There are no, or hardly any, restrictions with time or script. If Eric ad-libbed they could both run with it with no producer or director pulling them back. Ernie, being almost able to read Eric's mind, would instantly fall in line and go along with it, making it seem like they had written and rehearsed it.

Eric would often walk to the theatre before the show just to look around and get a feel for the place. Maybe it helped him to absorb the atmosphere, to get into the groove (as the younger generation describe it), or maybe he just wanted to have a walk! If Eric saw something during one of his pre-show rambles, he could bring it into the act on the night, sometimes without telling Ernie, but he knew whatever he did, it would not faze his partner. Ernie, despite being labelled the straight man, was just as quick as Eric but knew and accepted that whatever laugh there was to be had, it would be funnier coming from Eric.

By the seventies they were at the top of their profession, pulling in millions of viewers, especially for their much-anticipated Christmas shows. Although the shows were recorded in front of a live audience, there was something about performing to a packed house away from the cameras that drew them back time and time again. It wasn't nerves, definitely not. Ever since I knew him he was supremely confident working live, I think he believed in himself. Maybe this wasn't the case in his early days, but from the late sixties onwards, I never saw any nerves.

The walks turned into a routine he got into and he would often meet people connected with the venue and have a chat. It could be Mavis the cleaner, Fred the man sweeping the corridors, or Betty the lady in the ticket booth. He relished talking to people and I'm sure he would pick up on little things they all did and build them into a character or a routine.

When a show was on I would drive Eric to the theatre on the day of the event. He and Ernie would do a run through, more to help the stagehands and lighting people than themselves. They knew every aspect of their act, but understood and helped theatre staff who changed the set up for every single act on a weekly, sometimes daily basis. They would sort out the lighting, how long to wait for gags, make-up (what little they used) and markers.

An example of this can actually be seen in the 1978 episode of *The Sweeney* that they appeared in. They are seen running through the ventriloquist routine, and Eric informs someone off camera that the lights should black out on a given line.

Once there and before the show had actually started Eric would check his clothes. He usually took two suits for each appearance, one for the first house and one for the second. Shirts, shoes, jackets and ties. Props also had to be checked and placed ready to be picked up or handed over, and they carried quite a lot of them. If you have ever seen one of their live shows, or even viewed the video *Eric & Ernie Live*, you will see:

- The brown paper bag, usually in Eric's jacket pocket.
- A letter, used in several routines to represent a note from an angry fan, the BBC or Eric's mother.
- A handkerchief.
- Bongos, usually offstage to begin with.
- Paper cup for the Jimmy Durante gag.
- A tambourine (that didn't work).
- Bells with and without clappers.
- A cymbal and some maracas.
- And of course Charlie, the ventriloquist doll.

All had to be checked for damage, cleaned if necessary, and placed ready to be used at the given moment. Imagine if Eric walked out on stage, felt inside his pocket for the paper bag and it wasn't there!

Charlie, the doll, was my responsibility, I had him maintained, cleaned, oiled and ready to use for every show. He had his fair share of damage during the years, some easier to fix than others. Legs and arms would fall off, wigs would need replacing and fixing on, strings and levers had to be replaced. Having seen how he was treated during the live shows, you would know why this work was almost constant.

Charlie was not a one-off, he wasn't unique. There are, or were, at least another two dolls, almost identical. One was specially made for the American trip, to be used on the Ed Sullivan shows. Eric didn't want to risk losing him on the flight so had a second one made. He also had another made just for The Sweeney episode, again because he didn't want to lose or damage the original. It was strange, but Eric had these made so that Charlie number one wouldn't get broken, have you seen the way Eric knocked him about on stage? He gets slapped and punched, his head is rotated and pulled out and his limbs are crossed, pulled and swung around for about fifteen minutes each show. That's a lot of punishment for a small fella!

The relationship between a ventriloquist and their dolls can sometimes be very personal, and even though Eric was always very careful with Charlie (offstage), he didn't mind handing him over to me after the show. He was always kept in a large blue sack; even to this day, Charlie is transported in the same sack. Recently during a visit to Morecambe, Gary, Eric's son, noticed something odd about this sack and upon digging deeper found an original 1970s poster of Des O'Connor, folded up in the bottom. No doubt used at some stage by Eric to poke fun at his show business friend.

In contrast, Ray Alan, a great ventriloquist, whose doll was of course Lord Charles, was very particular about who handled his dummy. He would always have his wife there to hand Lord Charles over as he walked on stage, and to hand him back to when he left. On the rare occasion his wife wasn't there and he was playing the same theatre as Eric and Ernie, I would be trusted to take charge; a great honour. Maybe that should have been another career I could have considered, a sort of Geppetto to the stars!

The running order of the average live Morecambe and Wise show hardly changed, with Eric and Ernie being the main act coming on last. Usually starting off the show would be a ventriloquist act (like Ray Alan) or sometimes a tumbling act. Billing was usually given in order of importance, with the most famous coming further down the list. This was to allow the new acts to be seen, as you had to sit through the first half waiting for the top of the bill people later. Some of the wonderful and strange acts are now lost to history, whilst others you may have heard of. Here is a typical line up for one of the Bank Raids.

- Derek (and sometimes his wife) – Guitar and singing act.

- Lorna Dallas – A lovely singer.
- The Karlins – Three female singing sisters, two of them twins.
- Albert Seveen and Daisy May – The live talking dog.
- Keith Harris and Chuckles – Orville came much later.
- Arthur Tolcher – The mouth organ player who later appeared on the Morecambe and Wise shows.
- The Beverley Sisters.
- Pearl Carr and Teddy Johnson.
- Morecambe and Wise.

Walking about backstage was a strange experience, with all these people hanging around chatting or warming up. Sometimes theatres didn't have enough dressing rooms or the performers just wanted to chat to friends. The dusty stairways and well-trodden corridors were awash with noise. Albert Seveen could be heard barking like a dog and then shouting back at himself to shut up. Keith Harris would be testing his dummy and voices, dancers and acrobats would be limbering up and there would be lots of chatter and laughter echoing about.

Albert Seveen was a ventriloquist with a slightly different approach. He didn't use a dummy for his main character; instead it was a real dog called Mickey. Alongside Mickey was a dummy dog, used to tease the real one. He also had a schoolgirl doll called Daisy May.

The dummy dog would bark at Mickey, who just sat there, statue-like. Eventually Mickey would open its mouth and tell the dummy, "sharrr urrrp", much to the audience's amazement. The dog's mouth would open and close as Albert threw his voice. He was very secretive about how his dog could talk, everyone knew he was a ventriloquist and threw his voice, but how did the dog move its mouth? The secret, and don't say you heard it from me, was that the dog had a false bottom jaw cleverly made to look like the real thing. It was moulded and coloured to match Mickey's head and it was operated by Albert himself. Onstage, some distance from the audience, it was enough to fool everyone; he wanted to keep it that way too, never letting on to anyone how it was done. Only those who watched from backstage or got close enough could see the real truth.

Roy Hudd once told me he telephoned Albert about a show only to get the voice of Daisy May informing him her master was not available and to call back in 15 minutes. Roy said, "Come on Albert, it's me." But got the same reply. He hung up and called back in 15 minutes and this time Albert answered in his own voice and continued as though everything was normal!

In the early days, Arthur Tolcher (he of the famous *Not Now Arthur* catchphrase), was always quite high up on the cast list. If you go a little further back he was actually above Morecambe and Wise. He was an extraordinary player and his speciality was the one-inch mouth organ with just eight notes. He had worked with most of the top acts throughout his life, but had never managed to make it big himself. He was a wonderful man who would do anything he could to help fellow performers. He would often arrive in a town that Eric and Ernie were due to play to suss out the area and get the names of places that they could use in the act. Performers still use that trick, even today. They will slip in place names to get that familiarity with an audience. He would also check out local hotels in case there were problems with the official ones, so we could move if needed. He knew all the places to stay in every town; he had been touring them since he was a young teenager.

As variety theatres closed he found it difficult to get work, and asked Eric and Ernie if he could do a spot on their now well-watched television shows. They instantly agreed, but used him as a comical prop, whereby he never actually got to play, and the phrase, 'Not now Arthur,' was added to the list of popular quotes. As he became more famous for not playing when he appeared on television, he would often be the surprise guest on the Bank Raids. We had to make sure no one saw him going to the theatre and then hide him away somewhere until the end when he could get on stage, raise his mouth organ only to hear the shout from the wings. The audiences loved it.

Another surprise guest Eric and Ernie had in later years was Janet Webb. She was the large lady who appeared at the end of the BBC television shows taking the applause and claiming the show as her own. She didn't say a word until series five, and then we got to hear the words she used at the end of the live shows;

"I'd like to thank all of you for watching me and my little show here tonight. If you've enjoyed it, then it's all been worthwhile. So, until we meet again, goodnight, and I love you all."

She too would have to be sneaked in and hidden; easier said than done considering her size.

Arthur had always loved to be involved in live shows. He performed during the same period as Eric and Ernie, and they often toured together as youngsters. He enjoyed being involved in the business, no matter how big or small his part was, Janet on the other hand soon tired of the live work.

I can see her point (I'm sure Eric would have interjected with a joke here!). She would have to be at the theatre by 5pm so no one saw her arrive. She would then be stowed away somewhere in a room for hours on end with nothing to do and no one to talk to. At the end of the show, sometimes 11pm, she would walk on, do her bit and then leave. All that effort and boredom for just four minutes of work. She was paid well for it, but after a while she stopped doing it, and who could really blame her.

All the other acts came on and did their various routines before the short interval. The audience would get drinks and ice creams and slowly the tension would build. Next on, and for the next 40 to 45 minutes it would be Morecambe and Wise; the stars they had actually come to see. It often went on longer, particularly if it was second house, then the show could last well over an hour.

As the public settled back into their seats, clutching the food of choice, the backstage activity began to pick up. Checking the props one last time – four minutes – checking flies – three – running order – two – everyone ready – one – music... Finally Johnny Wiltshire and his band launched into an exaggerated version of *Bring Me Sunshine* and Eric and Ernie strolled on to the stage. The audience roared at the sight of their heroes. I ran through things in my head as I watched from the wings. Which props in what order, towels and water ready, Charlie sat patiently waiting for his limbs to be pummelled, concentrate. Even though I was working, I still remember it so clearly; the incredible applause, the ad-libs making each show just that little bit different, my important, unseen role. The audience quietened down and the act started.

> Ernie: Introduce me. I'm going to sing.
> Eric: You're not are you? And it's going so well.
> Ernie: Yes I am. Introduce me. Britain's answer to Frank Sinatra.
> Eric: (under his breath) More like Nancy Sinatra.
> Eric: Ladies and gentlemen, boys and girls. My partner will now sing a song. A song that has made him what he is today… (pause)… How do you spell… (raspberry)…?

The band kick in with the music. Eric and Ernie walk towards the microphone. Ernie approaches and as the music soars, he opens his mouth to sing…

> Eric: Great! Have you got anymore like that?
> (puts his arm around Ernie's shoulder and slaps his cheek)
> Ernie: Yes. But not quite as long.
> Eric: A bit louder maybe?
> Ernie: Yes, that could be arranged.

The band strike up again, both of them approach the microphone and get ready to sing. As they both open their mouths, all the lights go out.

Two spotlights illuminate Eric and Ern on stage.

Eric: It looks like two motorbikes coming towards you doesn't it?

Ernie begins to sing and the show is underway. Out comes the paper bag much to the delight of the audience. Eric throws an imaginary ball to someone in the audience who returns it back towards the waiting bag.

Ernie: Will you stop playing with that bag.
Eric: It's not a bag. It's a fella. What are you talking about?

More joking, crosstalk and a few names dropped thanks to his pre-show walks and then the first song, usually *Pretty Baby*. The music began and they both burst into song, often accompanied by a dance routine, depending on the song of course. Towards the end, they walked off stage as the music runs on. I'm there by the side of the stage, just out of view, waiting with towels and water. A quick wipe, a mouthful of water, Charlie handed over and Eric is straight back on stage for the ventriloquist routine.

If the song was, *Me And My Shadow* instead of *Pretty Baby*, then I would play a bigger part in the show. As they walked up and down doing the song, I would be backstage, just behind the curtains. As Eric and Ernie walked past, I would open the curtains slightly so Eric would vanish behind them leaving Ernie on stage alone. The audience loved that part. As Ernie came back, Eric would rejoin him for the end and then exit stage right where I would be again with towels, water and Charlie.

When they did the bongo routine, I was also involved in that, but sadly this was not seen in the live video, because there were no curtains on the stage. The live video, *Eric & Ernie Live*, is testament to how good they were with a live audience and was filmed at Fairfield Halls in Croydon. Sadly it is only available on VHS video second-hand, but well worth getting. Back to the bongos and Eric would stand with his back to the curtains, bongos between his knees ready to play. Ernie shouted and would beckon him to the front of the stage. Eric would look up and moved away to approach Ernie; as he did, it was my job to grab the bongos from behind the curtain so that they remained suspended on their own. It always got a huge laugh, and in a way that was me. I can honestly say, I have grabbed Eric's bongos on many occasions. Now that's not something you hear every day is it?

Even though the shows lasted between 45 minutes and an hour, that was by no means the end of things for Eric and Ernie. There could be fifty autograph books waiting for them and over a hundred fans all queuing up with things to be signed. On rare occasions some fans would be allowed in to the dressing room to see the boys and have a quick chat, and even some fool would try to be funny and outwit Eric. I felt sorry for these people as I had seen it many times before and knew what was coming. They usually left in a daze not knowing what had hit them; you could never top Eric, even when he was exhausted from doing a 45-minute show.

As throughout their career, the fans ranged from schoolchildren to pensioners and included all walks of life. Eric enjoyed talking to them all, for him that was part of the show, it was his way of thanking them. Ernie sometimes left early leaving Eric surrounded by cameras and autograph books. There must be loads of great pictures out there.

The places we visited during the raids all have memories, some faded, some lost, but some still strong today as ever. They played all corners of the country from Portsmouth to Newcastle, Manchester to Paignton; most were easy places to play, some, like Chichester were not.

The Chichester theatre had a semicircular stage with the audience on both sides and to the front. A very hard layout to play for a comedian, you have to address the audience, but with that layout, someone will always be left out and just see the back of your head. Eric and Ernie's comedy often included visual gags, the paper bag being a good example, but not as funny if all you can see is Eric's back.

The theatre also had no curtains, so things like the bongo routine and *Me and My Shadow* were impossible. The stage entrance was back-centre and because the orchestra was not on stage (they were in the orchestra stalls) the vent routine was made hard because Ernie couldn't hide anywhere. If you are not familiar with the routine, Eric is a bad ventriloquist and Ernie offers to help him out by doing the voice of the dummy. Ernie would hide, usually in the orchestra or behind a piano, and would try to fill in the voice as Eric ran through the usual stuff.

"Hello Charlie. How are you tonight?"

"I'm very well thank you."

"And what are you going to do for us tonight?"

With Ernie hidden, he couldn't see Eric operating the doll, which caused the timings to go out, so you got;

"Hello Charlie. How…"

"I'm very well thank you."

"…and what are…"

"I'm going to sing you a song."

Ernie's voice coming not only at the wrong time but also when the dummy's mouth was not moving; much to the annoyance and confusion of Eric, and the delight of the audience.

Because there were no wings; areas off stage to both sides; I also had difficulty in seeing the boys for the times I had to provide audio effects such as the tambourine and bell routine. When Ernie hit Eric and the sound of a bell was heard, that was me backstage, trying to get the timings right. Chichester made that part very hard.

Other places hold different memories; Oxford, of which there is more later, Peterborough ABC – the only venue that wasn't sold out on one occasion! Cambridge – a hall that resembled a gym! Bedworth Community Hall in which Eric famously ad-libbed, "I've never worked in an aircraft hangar before". Some of the venues remind me of specific events and just naming the location doesn't do them justice so what follows is a series of short anecdotes that stand out for me.

Chapter 9 – The Bank Raid Memoirs

Oxford and Keys

Oxford may mean many things to many people and I guess the word university would pop into most people's heads. For me though it is a completely different word; keys!

On this particular day we were up early preparing for the trip, packing all of the equipment, checking the car and making sure we hadn't left anything behind. Once happy we set off on what was a pleasant enough drive and we arrived in good time. Although it was a relaxing journey, Eric felt a little tired and said he would take a little nap once we had settled in. We checked-in and made sure the rooms were OK before we met back downstairs in the hotel's bar for some refreshments.

After a quick drink Eric excused himself and headed to his room at which point I decided to use the time to drop off the props at the theatre. I finished my drink and headed back to the Rolls in the hotel's car park. I am sure had anyone seen me making that innocent little walk I could have easily been arrested for some depraved act. It wasn't intentional and you don't think at the time, but I was just eager to find the keys and as such had my hands deep in my pockets and was fumbling around for quite a while. By the time I reached the car, I still hadn't located the keys and was starting to get worried, it was a decent distance and I only had two pockets. Where had I left them? I'm sure I hadn't dropped them or put them down in my room, or left them at the bar. I was always careful; it was my job after all. I don't know why people do this but I'm sure I am not alone, but I checked my pockets again knowing full well they contained no keys.

All two pockets now fully explored several times, I was stood by the driver's door, mind blank and the beginning of panic swirling around in my stomach. I then did what most people do when looking for something; and there is no logical reason why they do it. I turned around slowly and looked in every direction. Even though I knew I had never been in that part of the car park, I still squinted in the vain hope of seeing them. I must have looked like a car thief, sizing the place up. Another chance to get arrested; that would have been twice in an hour!

Was I looking for the keys, some kind of heavenly intervention or just help? Whichever it was something must have worked. It was while I was standing there doing my impression of a lighthouse that my madness paid off, and I spotted them. Not on the floor, not even in the car park, you guessed it; they were dangling there, in the ignition. As I stared in disbelief, thinking what a fool I had been, I'm sure I saw them wink at me.

The Rolls had a central locking system that was either activated by locking the driver door, or by the method I had used which was to push down the button on the door and slam it shut. This meant the keys were now securely locked inside and I was embarrassingly locked out. Even though I knew all of the doors would be locked, I tried them all, several times. Well, you do don't you? I even searched my pockets again, I have no idea why humans do this, it must be some kind of last desperate effort and that by magic, another set of keys would slide their way in there. They didn't, and I was still locked out.

Looking at my watch it was then I realised the fullness of the problem. There was only an hour to go before the show and all of the equipment was firmly sealed in the boot; poor Charlie, not only stuffed inside a bag but now locked in a boot as well! Eric on the other hand was asleep and blissfully unaware of my rapidly raising heart rate. There was nothing else to do but panic. That sadly didn't work and so it was back to trying other methods to solve this problem. Whatever I did I had to make sure Eric didn't find out, I would look such a fool and he would not be pleased, I had to find a way out of this before he woke up and came looking for me. Running out of options and not really wanting to smash a window I swallowed my pride and called Joan, his wife. We arranged for a friend of mine to pick up the spare set from her and rush them over to me in Oxford. Joan, I suspect, had a huge grin on her face, knowing that I was stuck in a car park going mad while Eric slept quietly. Now all I had to do was wait.

Why is it that when you are waiting for something time seems to slow down. You could swear 20 minutes had gone by but your watch says one! So there I stood, loitering next to a Rolls Royce; that must be the third arrest so far! During the painfully long wait I did what any normal man would do. I prowled around the car looking for ideas of how to get in. Trying the doors again, this time tugging a bit harder, trying to pull the windows down with your fingers, trying the boot lid; everything.

Another man, who must have sneaked in while I was looking underneath the car noticed my predicament and came over to lend a hand. The simplest of things slip your mind when you panic, so the thought of using the tried and trusted coat hanger never entered my head. This man wasn't panicking though and had a clear head. Within ten minutes we were poking the wire in trying to loop it over the catch. I have no idea where the actual coat hanger came from, and I didn't ask. I was just happy that with time running out, we were at last a little closer to getting into the car.

It wasn't easy trying to lasso the catch but eventually to my relief there was a loud click and the door swung open. I quickly grabbed the keys and glared at them. I felt like holding them above my head like some kind of trophy, but quickly dispelled that idea; I had already made an idiot of myself, no point in making it worse. I thanked the person for helping me, and he quickly left, taking his coat hanger with him. As I stood there basking in my victory it suddenly dawned on me that my friend was still on his mission to get the spare set to me.

With mobile phones some years away, I had to rush back to the hotel to try and catch him before he had left. Even though I was a lot faster than I am now, I wasn't fast enough and he had left, the thought of being the hero of the hour no doubt in his mind as he undoubtedly drove faster than he should so that the show would not be delayed. He was a bit disappointed to have made that trip for nothing, but as a thank you I got him to help me unload the props. He was really pleased with that! To make it up to him, I got him in the theatre to watch the show.

During all this confusion and panic, Eric slept on. I never told him and unless Joan had a quiet word, I think he never found out. Although knowing him, even if he did know, he wasn't the type to mention it, thank goodness. Probably saving it for a special day when he could use it to great comic effect and heighten my embarrassment. Sadly that day never came.

Brighton Seafood

It was a one-night only, whistle-stop Bank Raid in Brighton. We would travel up there in the morning, do the show and then come back late at night. We had to do this because Eric had something on for the following day. Often if the following day was free, we might stay over, but not on this particular day. Luckily back then, the roads were not that busy, especially at night, which was to our advantage, as we had to use the dreaded A23 Brighton Road and over Vauxhall Bridge.

After the show there were the usual autograph hunters and queues of people, and one man who I will always remember. He was the manager of Wheelers Seafood Restaurant, famous for its shellfish.

Eric loved seafood and we arranged to pick up some free offerings on the way back, so he could eat them during the journey. Sure enough a bag of fresh seafaring snacks were brought to the car, and with Eric rummaging around like a kid with a bag of sweats, we headed off.

As I drove I could hear shells being broken and the, 'Mmmm, mmmm,' sound as each piece was tasted and approved. I could also smell them; a car is not an ideal place to eat seafood so we opened the windows. This helped with the smell and also gave Eric a convenient way of discarding the bits he didn't eat. All the way up the M25 he was munching away, hurling bits of crab, and prawn shells out of the back windows. I have no idea what anyone would have thought if they saw us. A Rolls Royce scattering scraps of seafood all over the road.

Torquay and Tommy

Another Friday and another Bank Raid. This time it was in the lovely resort of Torquay with sun, sea and 'kiss me quick' hats. The holidaymakers were mainly the older generation, but there was still a healthy gathering of the younger end too.

Eric and Ernie had four shows to do over the weekend and as we arrived we noticed that there was another famous comic in town too; Tommy Cooper. He was there for the summer season and every one of his shows had sold out. Eric, Ernie and Tommy went back years, back to the fifties, and they were old friends. They have met up before socially and the events usually ended in riots of laughter. Can you imagine Eric and Tommy together, each trying to outdo the other in a restaurant!

When they meet, they relax and let the jokes flow. There is no pressure, but inside I think they held private competitions. There was no winner, there was no one keeping score; everyone was far too busy laughing to care. Eric roared at Tommy's one-liners and comic mishaps and at the same time Tommy cried with laughter as Eric shot him sideways glances and fired back equally funny quips.

"Shall we get the waiter?"

"I was thinking of the chicken – I've heard about people like you!"

"Roast parsnips?"

"I didn't know they cooked those bits?"

"He is walking funny..."

Before Tommy's show, Eric, along with Joan and myself decided to visit him in his dressing room. Despite the amounts of alcohol he drank, he was in top form and virtually did his full act, right there in the room. My ribs ached with laughter. Tommy was just one of those very rare people who are just funny. There is no reason to it, you can't learn it, you can't gain it, you are either born with it, like Tommy and Eric, or you aren't.

What a night. Two naturally born funny men, in the same tiny dressing room, rolling around with laughter. Something I will never forget and something I shall always miss.

Paignton Pleasantries

Just around the coast from Torquay is Paignton, Devon. Eric and Ernie were playing there and after one show I was leaving the stage door and accidentally bumped into a holidaying family. No harm was done and no one sued me for reckless meandering, but we got chatting and I discovered they lived a few doors away from Eric in Harpenden. When Eric found out, he came out for a chat and as ever was always happy to engage with his fans. They didn't know the boys were playing until the last minute, by which time there were no tickets left. In fact the show had been sold out for over six weeks.

Eric was having none of it and soon secured 'house' seats for them. These were seats left available until the very last minute in case any celebrities or dignitaries decided they wanted to visit. The family were over the moon and got to watch Eric and Ernie at their very best, in front of a packed audience. This was how Eric was. Very accommodating, very friendly and always happy to give back. Something that sadly can't be said of many of today's 'celebrities'.

Southampton Shenanigans

Southampton always brought a smile to Eric's face; it was yet another excuse to use a rather old joke on Ernie.

> Eric: Ern, we're in Southampton. We're staying at the dead parrot.
> Ernie: Don't be stupid. There's no such hotel.
> Eric: There is. At least that's what I call it.
> Ernie: What you call what?
> Eric: The Polygon.

Southampton on the other hand always brings a feeling of 'what could have been' to me.

Eric and I were in his dressing room preparing for the evening show. He was relaxing while I checked the paper bag and gave Charlie a last minute polish. He pulled out his pipe, that was Eric and not Charlie, and after searching unsuccessfully for a match, asked me for light. I found a box of matches, opened it up, pulled out a match and lit it up. A few clouds of smoke later I blew out the match and surveyed the room for an ashtray. This was years before the smoking ban and so it was usual for rooms to have ashtrays. I couldn't see one so not wanting to litter the dressing room; I just popped the match back into the box.

There then followed what I can only explain as a small explosion. The match, still hot, ignited the others and I found myself now holding a small blazing fireball and wondering what the hell I should do with it. With time not on my side I dropped it, cursing under my breath and wafting my hands about wildly.

Eric sat and watched, puffing away on his pipe as the box fell to the floor where it proceeded to set fire to the carpet. Things were not going well. I have no idea what was going through Eric's mind, but I was just a little worried at this point. No doubt he was calmly taking it all in and building some sketch about it while I rushed about like a maniac. Hastily I stomped out the flames and looked around for something to cover the smouldering hole. Finding nothing we embarrassingly decided to leave it there for posterity. We could always blame it on the other acts.

As we left Eric looked down at it with a rueful smile;

"I should sign that," he said. "People would pay to see that. This place could make a fortune."

We left quietly.

The Rhyl Limp

Like a lot of theatres by the sea, the one at Rhyl was right on the seafront. We had got there in good time as usual, and went to set things up and check out the lighting and props. As we entered the place we were immediately hit by the most horrendous smell. It was a mixture of smells, all of which emanated from the rear ends of various animals. Now in the old days theatres always had a smell to them, it was part of the atmosphere. Sometimes it would be stale smoke or a damp, musty smell seeping up from the cellars, but not this time.

It turned out the week previously, there had been a circus there and when they had left, they hadn't quite managed to take everything with them. The whole theatre stank of, well, you know what, and every door and window was wide open to try and clear it. Eric pondered the situation, but not for very long. We decided to leave the gear in the boot of the car, take a stroll on the seafront and hope that they managed to get it cleared before the evening show.

Being in high season the resort was packed, especially there on the seafront. The chances of Eric not being spotted were very high, and although he loved meeting fans, this was 'his' time before the show to relax. Again he pondered before finally smiling and chuckling to himself. He winked at me, took off his glasses and put on a flat cap, one of the props he had brought from the car. As we left the theatre he began to limp and for the whole walk not a single person recognised him. It's amazing how something like a pair of glasses can become so iconic, and once removed, people just don't make the connection.

As the show grew closer, our return to the theatre made it clear that despite all of their efforts, the crew had failed to completely rid the place of the smell. It was too late to cancel, and Eric would not have done that anyway, so the show went on. The boys walked on and Eric addressed the issue straight away.

"I'd like to thank you all for coming… to the zoo. At least I think it's a zoo, it's either that or the mushy peas Ern had last night. I knew the sea air is meant to do you good, but come on…"

Sneaky Scarborough

It was the day after the show in Scarborough and Eric was staying at the lovely North Yorkshire Moors National Park Hotel. It was peaceful there, and Eric could sit by the lake watching the wildlife and slowly wind down.

After a breakfast of kippers, we set off home when Eric suddenly mentioned he fancied a drink. He blamed the kippers, and who was I to disagree. By this time we were now in York and managed to find a nice looking place just near the racecourse. It was just right for Eric; empty. After a show, and in-between hoards of fans, he would find time to be quiet and relax, to recharge and be himself without the need to be funny. It's not that he didn't like the fans, far from it, as you will have already read; he loved them, and knew if it weren't for them, he and Ernie would not be in their position as top entertainers. It was just now and again he fancied some quiet time, as we all do, to slow down and take a breath.

I ordered some drinks, which the management very kindly offered on the house, and we sat back and raised the glasses at our success for finding such a place. As the glasses touched our lips, over the rims we both saw a coach pull into the car park. This was quickly followed by another, and finally a third, all full of W.I. women. That would be over a hundred women, all no doubt fans and all thrilled that Eric was sat there. I looked at Eric and he stared back at me with a look of 'Hellfire' on his face. We only wanted a quiet drink after all and the place was about to be invaded. The coach doors opened and out poured excited women, chatting and laughing, unaware that just a few yards away two men were looking for an escape route.

Luckily the barman had also seen the coaches and very probably the look on our faces. He came over and quickly ushered us into an empty room where we could finish our drinks in peace. We took our seats as the invading forces of the W.I. poured in and turned our quiet little rest into a madhouse of chatter and laughter.

We finished our drinks and I casually strolled through the now heaving bar and out to the car. No one recognised me and I am surprised no one took any notice of the Rolls as I climbed in. She started first time, as usual, and I pulled round to the back doors where Eric had been guided through the kitchen and now waited. He jumped in and we drove off leaving the W.I. blissfully unaware of how close they were.

This was a very rare occasion when he didn't want to meet his fans. It was just one of those days when he wanted to be alone. We all get them, and it just proves he was like everyone else. In fact I think he sneakily enjoyed giving them the slip, he had a smile on his face for the rest of the day.

Newcastle Nonsense

The boys had been playing Newcastle upon Tyne and the following morning Eric and I set off in the Rolls for home. There was no rush and with Eric in the front seat we cruised along enjoying the scenery. It was a few minutes into the journey that I noticed the blue flashing light of a police car in the rear mirror. They were quite far back so I was not really concerned and continued as normal. As they got closer I moved over to the left-hand lane and waited for them to pass; they didn't.

All drivers get that little niggling feeling when they see a police car, and all of the usual thoughts went through my mind. Had I updated the tax? Had I checked the tyres? Was something wrong with the car? Did they hear about the seafood incident from fellow officers?

The police car was soon at the side of us and glancing across I noticed one of the occupants was waving for us to pull over. Eric had also seen this.

"What have you done now?" he asked.

"Nothing. I was only doing forty!"

"There must be something wrong with the car then."

We pulled over and stopped.

"Another fine mess you've got me into!" he quipped as we stopped.

The policeman approached and Eric pressed the button to lower the window. I held my breath, hoping it would be something small like an indicator was not working. Even though I knew the car was in perfect working order and that I had been driving within the legal limits, it didn't stop me worrying. The window slid down and the officer poked his head through;

"Could I have your autograph please Mr. Morecambe?"

Eric and I exchanged glances as the officer continued, holding out a piece of paper.

"We spotted Mr. Wise earlier and managed to get his. He told us you had left the hotel and that you would be using this road."

Eric signed the piece of paper and handed it back, no doubt cursing his partner and promising himself he would get his own back one day. With his autograph in his hand the officer walked back to his car and we were allowed to continue with our journey. He had managed to get us before we had left his area, but only because of the blue lights!

The Great Yarmouth Miracle

Many people have claimed to have witnessed miracles, and I can honestly say that I am one of them.

Morecambe and Wise were alternating their shows between Bournemouth and Great Yarmouth, playing every other Sunday in each location. Because it was a summer season, we had to drive the same route over and over again. With this in mind I often tried to change routes so that things didn't get too repetitive.

On this particular day Eric and I were heading back from Yarmouth, and as usual, Eric was relaxing after his kipper breakfast. I had chosen to take the scenic route and we were in open farmlands with countryside all around.

"When and if you can find a nice pub," Eric said, "we'll have a drink. Those kippers again."

A little further along and sure enough, a small, olde worlde pub came into view with an empty car park. Perfect. I pulled into the car park and parked up opposite the door just in case we needed to make another quick getaway. Eric asked if I would go in and check the place out. I agreed and left him in the car hoping the W.I. were not in the vicinity. I walked the few yards to the door and peered inside. Sure enough it was empty, but it looked like a party was in progress and all the people had mysteriously vanished. There were empty bottles crowded on every table and all the ashtrays were overflowing. It had obviously been left that way from the previous night, and was waiting to be cleaned.

I walked to the bar and explained to the lady of mature years stood there, that I had Eric Morecambe in the car outside, and would it be alright if we came in for a drink. I could see the look of panic in her eyes.

"Certainly," she said, glancing round at the state of the place, "Just give me a few minutes."

I strolled back to the car, not knowing how Eric would react if he decided to go in. I informed Eric that the place was empty but the ashtrays were not. I also told him about the tables, the empty bottles, the stale smell and he still didn't seem too bothered. Finally I gave in and together we headed back to the door for our quick drink.

To this day I have no idea how that lady did it, but when we entered, the place was spotless. All the bottles had gone, the ashtrays were empty and the place was clean. It was like a different pub. Eric came in and looked around and then quizzically at me. All I could do was shrug. What else could I do? I had seen the mess with my own eyes, I didn't imagine it, but now it was gone. Stood at the bar was a smiling lady who wasn't even out of breath.

We ordered our drinks and Eric happily chatted to the lady, no doubt trying to find out her secret, or indeed if I was seeing things. With Eric still convinced I was going mad, we left. I am still bemused as to how she managed it. I could have done with some tips from her, especially with my ever-expanding role in the Morecambe household.

The Bournemouth Contraption

Because of the workload and the demands for Eric and Ernie it would often mean working at different location on alternate weekends. Great Yarmouth one weekend and then over to Bournemouth for the next, then back to Yarmouth for a second show.

This particular week as we headed to Bournemouth Eric had heard that Norman Wisdom was playing the theatre opposite and asked if I would mind paying him a visit. Of course I was delighted and so once we had arrived, unpacked and sorted out the hotels and Eric's theatre, we walked across the road to the Winter Gardens in search of Norman.

We checked the dressing rooms, stage, wings, everywhere, but he wasn't to be found. As we passed by the stage I noticed a strange contraption to one side. It was quite large, painted black and red and consisted of various things all stuck together. A large hammer was suspended above what looked like a toilet seat, a cymbal was hung on one side and on the other was a large drum. Beneath the cymbal was a pedal that obviously worked this thing, but what it was for neither myself nor Eric had the faintest idea.

Failing to find Norman or figure out this contraption, we headed back to the theatre across the car park. As we got about halfway a man approached us as though he knew us. I immediately thought it must be a fan but it turned out to be Jimmy Tarbuck out for a stroll. Eric, Jimmy and I chatted for a while before at last getting back to the hotel.

Many years later, in fact in 2011, the mystery of the contraption was finally solved. I was watching a DVD of Norman Wisdom called *Trouble On Tour* and there it was, on stage. It was one of his props and provided a rather typical Wisdom routine about confusion and consequence. Strange how these things lodge in your mind and you forget about them, only to have them suddenly pop back up at the most unexpected moment. I had all but forgot our trip to find Norman and our meeting with Jimmy, but as he worked the audience using this device as a stooge, the memories and the mystery came back.

Chapter 10 – At Home With The Morecambes

You would have thought that I had my hands full keeping the cars in tip-top shape and actually driving them, but there was more to my role than chauffeur. My official job description was chauffeur/handyman. I'm not sure if that meant I had to be handy at driving, which I was; or that I was a handyman with a bit of driving on the side! Luckily it was a chauffeur, as my DIY skills have been described as many things, mainly uncomplimentary and mostly unpublishable, but the one thing they are not, is 'handy'.

Of my other roles, the one I enjoyed most was looking after the wonderful gardens that surrounded the house at Harpenden. That was no mean feat. The gardens covered about three quarters of an acre, with a large variety of plants and shrubs, not to mention the lawn and paths; all of which I had to clean, sweep, cut, trim and water.

It was lovely to spend a few hours in the garden, either alone or with Eric, especially if the weather was warm. Eric was not an enthusiastic gardener compared to fishing or birdwatching, but he liked to dabble with anything connected to nature. A gardening magazine somehow picked up on this and did a large spread about Eric and his garden. It really surprised me because he was not at all interested. They took photographs of him holding the handles of a wheelbarrow, which actually wasn't functional. It was a decorative one!

Another feature of the garden was his fish pond. Strangely, despite his love of fishing, he would also like to keep them as pets. He had a large indoor aquarium too, stocked with all kinds of brightly coloured fish, which had to be kept fed and cleaned whenever he and Joan went on holiday.

The outdoor pond, something else that I had to maintain, was kept well stocked with large koi carp, when they didn't mysteriously vanish! One of the largest koi we had, one day suddenly disappeared from the pond, causing all kinds of confusion and head scratching. Surely Eric hadn't suddenly decided to break out his tackle and pick off an easy one?

Eventually the fish was found where fish are rarely seen, the lawn! The limp carcass, complete with large hole, presumably caused by a heron, was found the following day. Luckily it was located before its now rather pungent body was sucked up into the lawnmower and scattered to the winds. I'm sure there is a comedy routine in there somewhere, like so many of Eric's ideas; it would have come from real life.

Continuing with the pet theme, Barney was also placed in my care. Barney was a large Labrador, golden retriever cross and like all dogs, needed a lot of exercise. You can't complain can you, being paid to walk through glorious countryside on a warm summer day, being dragged from tree to tree by the dog of Eric Morecambe. I spent most of my postman days trying to avoid the things for obvious reasons, and now, here I am, tethered to one! Is this some kind of canine payback? Luckily I get on well with most dogs, unlike my wife Lesley, who had a strange allergy to long-haired Labradors! Maybe it was just an excuse to get out of taking him out because she was fine with other dogs.

Barney was a good-natured animal though, quite different to his predecessor, Chippy. Chippy was a small terrier that had issues with, well with most things really. He was not badly behaved; he was like many of the people thrown up on talent shows in that he loved the sound of his own voice. The sad thing was, his voice was often far better than the aforementioned 'celebrities' and could usually be quietened with a sharp command. He also had some kind of reverse guard dog logic somewhere deep in his head. He would let people into the house with little more than a cautious glance, but trouble lay ahead if they ever wanted to leave.

I'm sure he could understand some words and phrases like, "I better be going now," and "I'll be on my way then". One minute he would be dozing on the carpet, suddenly the words would float across and wriggle into his ears. His eyes would flicker and focus and then he would go berserk. He would pounce into action, scurrying around guests' ankles, nipping and growling all the way to the door. Maybe he thought it didn't matter who came in as long as they didn't leave with anything, particularly their own feet!

In between gardening, fish and dog duties and cleaning the odd window, thirteen to be exact, there were always the cars and driving to attend to. A never-ending series of tasks for which I was paid and enjoyed. It was in fact whilst cleaning one of the cars that Eric noticed something odd about me, and decided to take immediate action, which I am very glad he did.

I had been having very bad indigestion for over a week prior to the event, and despite eating the local chemist out of Rennies, my wife Lesley had forced me to go to the doctors. He pondered the situation and calmly prescribed yet more pills.

A few more days past and the pain, although no longer constant, was still giving me some trouble, especially whilst stretching to clean the Rolls. Eric noticed this and asked if I was all right. I explained about the pain, the indigestion and joked that I was surprised he hadn't heard the large quantity of pills rattling about inside me. With a rather worried look on his face, he retreated back into the house and quickly called his private consultant and booked me in to see him the next day.

After the tests came back from Harefield Hospital, the consultant informed me that I had suffered a heart attack. Blimey, I nearly had another one I can tell you! I now know how Eric felt when he described his experience of his first attack, on *Parkinson*. You don't think it is something like that, but get quite a shock when you discover the truth.

More hastily arranged tests and results were conclusive; I had blocked arteries and needed immediate attention. Soon afterwards I was in hospital having an arterial bypass by Mr. Yacoub, the same surgeon that operated on Eric. In those days, it was not such a routine operation and I was hospitalised for three weeks. Who would clean the cars now? At the time I had only been married a few months, so this was a real traumatic time for my wife. She stayed in a bungalow provided by the hospital during the critical phase, and was very worried about the future. At the time my stepmother passed away too, just a few days before the operation. Lesley was advised not to tell me until afterwards; what a burden for a young bride.

It was Eric who had saved my life, something I so wish I could have done in return. He had seen me having difficulties and noticed something was not right. He could have easily ignored it, passed it off as just a strain or even indigestion. He didn't, that was not Eric; he always took an interest and always looked out for other people. Thanks to his quick actions I am here, the operation went well and after a few months I was back to work, bucket full of soapy water and a sponge in my hand, never happier.

It seems most of my working life I have either had a soapy sponge permanently attached to my right arm washing a car or sat inside one driving someone somewhere. I drove not only Eric and Joan, but his children too.

Gary, Gail and later Stephen, whom Eric and Joan adopted, all had to be taken to school. In a combined, military-like operation, the journeys and times had to be planned and executed like clockwork. Think about the logistics behind getting three children to three different schools at the same time. Somehow we managed and even enjoyed the journeys.

Stephen, when he was very young, would always make us laugh as we drove along, peering out of the window saying things like; "Look at the countwee twees." And, "Turn on the swind sween swipers." He was a lovely lad, Lesley and I often looked after him if Eric and Joan had to go away for something. Usually when this happened Stephen had to go to school and so we stayed at Eric's house. That way I could still do my handyman activities and Stephen could still go to school; house-sitting is the word I am fishing for. He was a fun-loving and active boy, who had a wicked sense of humour.

On one occasion during one of our house-sitting sessions when he would have been about ten, I had got up early. I made my way downstairs to the kitchen, put the kettle on and let Barney out in the garden. When I got back upstairs I noticed Stephen had sneaked into the bedroom and was lying on the bed next to Lesley, smiling. Lesley began to tickle him, and with howls of laughter they rolled about on the bed giggling like madmen. Things soon escalated and pillows were introduced into the fracas. Swiping, giggling and tickling, they moved from the bed into the room and headed into the hallway, pillows still whirling around their heads.

Something had to happen and sure enough with the kind of thud that often stops these things, a plate was dislodged from the wall and dropped. The pillows stopped in mid-air, everyone watched helplessly as this no doubt expensive ornament spun in slow motion and met the floor with another heart-stopping crack. It didn't survive, and was in numerous pieces as we all stood over it like something that had just been run over. No amount of staring seemed to work, so I picked it up, piece by piece and vainly tried to glue it all back together. I had all the right pieces, but could I get them back in the right order? Lesley was very worried. What if it was really expensive or a family heirloom? What if it was some kind of award, what if...?

Stephen, even though he was only ten, did what Eric and Joan have described several times; he showed how considerate and kind he was. He told us not to worry and that he would say it was him who had knocked it off by accident. This young lad was fully prepared to take the blame for us, should we allow this? Well... yes!

After my attempts to stick it back together we rehung it, and it was at this point we realised Stephen's cunning plan had a fatal flaw. He was only about four-feet high and the plate was positioned well above his reach on the wall. After some thought we decided to see what happened and left it there, blatantly broken, but only noticeable if you were looking at it! This plan worked and it remained there for several years, unnoticed. When it was finally discovered neither of us were there and it was just thrown out. Not priceless, not an heirloom and not an award; just some plate that probably everyone didn't like and wished it would break so they could throw it away!

Lesley and I loved to stay in Harpenden when Eric was away; it was almost like a holiday, at least for Lesley. I still had my duties, but even then, it was away from our home life. The sun would shine, we would sit out in the garden, Lesley telling me I'd missed a bit whilst mowing the lawn, pointing out some weeds that needed pulling, asking for more drinks, yes it was a real treat for me. At least we had the pool, which Eric always allowed us to use, even if they were there too. Often after a hot day in the garden or cleaning the cars, Joan would tell me to take a dip to cool off. There are several well-known photographs of Joan and Eric around the pool and if you look closely you can see me in the background, trying not to be seen.

Eric even allowed us to take our son, also called Steven, with us, and it was there, in Eric's garden, that he took his very first steps. A moment no parent ever forgets; made even more special by the wonderful location. Something we both will always remember.

My many and varied jobs around the Morecambe household were all a pleasure to do, apart from the weeding, which I think no one really likes. There were days when it often seemed I was working in a mini-museum, with Eric's numerous awards and artefacts from various shows scattered about. I felt privileged to be able to look at them close up, to touch them and to admire how much the public loved Eric, shown by these wonderful pieces. Some rekindled memories of these events, that I very often attended, at the insistence of Eric, or in the very least, drove him to them.

"Another one in the bag Michael." He would say, climbing into the Rolls clutching an award.

He didn't mock them, he didn't take them for granted. Everything he was ever given in recognition for his work he cherished. It was something to remind him why he put himself and his family through the tough times, and why he kept on going back. He wasn't a collector of awards, in that he didn't go out to make something that would win. He went out to make something to the best of his ability. He put everything in and if the public liked it, that was reward enough. To win something as well was just icing on the cake.

Eric had a lot of icing.

Chapter 11 – Contribution To Comedy

Some people knock the many and varied awards so vigorously handed out these days. It seems that if you don't win one, not to worry, because like buses, there will be another three along very soon. The whole awards thing has been watered down somewhat, and even the yearly honours handed out by the Queen often get criticised. But in 1976, to get such an award was a mark of achievement. It meant you had not only done something right, but you had done something exceptional.

By 1976, the Morecambe and Wise shows were topping the viewing figures and were watched by millions, especially the highly secretive Christmas shows. Unlike today where shows seem to centre around who will be on and how best to advertise the fact, the Morecambe and Wise Christmas show was almost the opposite. They didn't need to boast about which celebrity was to appear just to get an audience. Sometimes it seems to me that most of a television show is shown when advertising it. The highlights and sound bites are in the public domain way before the shows are seen and therefore there are no surprises.

People tuned in to watch Eric and Ernie, to see the Play What Ernie Wrote, to watch the dance numbers and to be entertained without foul language or political overtones. Yes, they had guests on but because it was kept secret, the excitement would grow as the time grew closer. Because of this and because it was a surprise, you were genuinely enthusiastic and it proved a great talking point both before and after the show. It helped get people watching because if you didn't see it you were the odd one out the following day when everyone else was talking about it.

It was because of this, and of course Eric and Ernie's continued work in entertainment, from radio to stage and television, that they were awarded the O.B.E. by one of their biggest fans, the Queen. The award was given, as is the custom, at Buckingham Palace. I had always liked it and had often seen it from the public side of the railings, but now I was to enter the home of Queen Elizabeth II.

Eric used to jest that he was to be awarded the O.B.E. – Old Butlins Entertainer, but he was really proud of the fact that he and Ern had been honoured. Like many top acts in those days, they had performed privately for the Queen, at luncheons and special events, but this was to be different, this was a private ceremony; a serious event. That of course didn't stop Eric's flow of one-liners.

Before all that though, we had to get there, which would prove difficult especially as everyone was really excited, even Eric. As anyone with a family will know, getting everyone organised and ready on time is almost impossible, and the one thing we couldn't do on this occasion was be late. Inside the house, Gail, Gary, Joan and Eric were in a frenzy of clothes and make-up. The usual last-minute doubts about what to wear and continuous grooming in front of the mirror. I, on the other hand, was outside with a cloth, giving the Rolls a last-minute polish.

As the time to leave grew closer I became aware of activity that didn't befit the day, it was a different kind of panic. On investigation I found the family running around trying to catch a dove that had mistakenly flown into the house and was flapping around like everyone else. Attention had turned from dresses, make-up and shoes to this wild bird desperately trying to get out of the house by randomly flying into windows.

The clock was ticking and now we were all focused on catching this thing before it did some harm to either itself, the house, or both. We couldn't leave it inside, and it seemed, after several meetings with the windows, to be injured. The next question that came into our heads was what to do with it if we caught it. We had an appointment with the Queen and there we were, all stood around, in various states of dress, staring at this bird wondering what to do. We eventually managed to corner it and pick it up. Suggestions were voiced about vets, the RSPCA, the garden, the cat…

"We should take it with us," Eric announced, "as a present."

We opted for an easier option and took it to the stables for safekeeping. Placing it in some fresh straw and closing the doors, we left it alone and turned our attention back to the job in hand; going to see the Queen. Everyone went back to hair straightening and clothes brushing before finally climbing into the Rolls, still discussing the bird and its future. It was something to take their minds off what was actually happening and where they were actually going.

Of the things people talk about when going to meet the Queen and to collect an award, the well-being of a dove is probably low on the list. It was still being discussed as we pulled up to the entrance.

"I still think we should have brought it," Eric insisted. "If she didn't like it she could put it in a pie."

Something that people may not be aware of when entering the Palace is the huge amount of security, both seen and unseen. You always knew someone was watching you even if you couldn't see them. It is the strangest feeling knowing your every move is being watched, I mean, what if you get an itch! Would someone sat in a room watching a monitor zoom in on your rapidly moving hand, getting a close up of that face you always pull when having a good scratch? Could you get arrested for it?

The other side of things, also probably not known, is the very strict protocol you must follow, even for us drivers. We are told how to drive, where to stop, where to park, how long to wait; it was like being back at school. We entered via the left arch with the crowds being pulled aside to allow the fleet of cars in. There is usually a small queue at these events, strictly controlled by the Palace so as not to have anyone waiting too long, it was all choreographed like one of Eric and Ern's dance routines.

Once in the courtyard I pulled up slowly in front of the main steps and waited. A page would appear, open the door and receive the guest. The door would close and I would then drive away to my designated parking slot outside of the Palace. Oh the dizzy heights I reached! Like all the other drivers, I had to remain in the car until called upon to collect the guests, so a packed lunch was important. You couldn't just nip off to the pub or sneak away for a burger. It seems to take an eternity when you're sat on your own in a Rolls Royce eating a cheese sandwich.

I used to switch the radio on or sometimes play one of the eight-track tapes Eric used to have. There was a nice little selection including Andy Williams, Glenn Miller, Shirley Bassey and various jazz and big band music. Matt Munro, Barbra Streisand and even Frank Zappa all used to make the wait more pleasurable, until the tannoy interrupted. The tannoy system was set up to inform the waiting drivers that they must now go back to the Palace and collect the guests. Again it was like military manoeuvres, all carefully planned and executed. The car pulled up by the steps, the page would reappear, open the door, Eric and family climbed back in, the door was closed and we moved off and headed home.

The O.B.E. was a little different though as the waiting press wanted interviews and Eric, not one to disappoint, stayed there answering questions for quite some time. It was a good job I brought two cheese sandwiches. I don't know if food was served, but looking at the faces of the rest of his family on the news coverage, it seems to me they just wanted to get home and eat.

If Eric had any nerves on the day, he didn't show them, and he obliged the waiting crowds with a stream of jokes and calmly gave interviews to various television and radio stations. It had, as it normally did with Eric, turned into another impromptu show as he and Ernie held out their awards and like true professionals, kept the jokes coming. At one point Eric swapped his O.B.E. for his wristwatch, and there are several photographs that appeared in the press of this. I wonder if they even noticed!

Eric, the family and even I were immensely proud that day. Typically Eric joked that it should have the M.B.E. – so he could boast – Morecambe's Best Entertainer.

Buckingham Palace was visited a fair few times, usually for charity events such as the "Goaldiggers", a charity connected to The Sun newspaper. Somehow the charity had persuaded four celebrities to record a special single to sell to help raise money. Elton John, Brian Moore, Jimmy Hill and Eric all put their voices to it and 500 were pressed ready to auction. The single 'The Goaldiggers Song' featured just Elton, but the B-side was the part where Eric and the others could be heard.

Initially they were all sold at auction before I had a chance to hear it and it wasn't until recently when a friend managed to track one down that I got the chance. They are, apparently, very collectable now, with people asking upwards of £350 for a copy! It was, as you can imagine a time of excitement for me to hear it at last after over 30 years.

With all the copies sold, the final cheque was to be handed over to the Duke of Edinburgh at the Palace. Jimmy and Eric were to hand it over and the staggering amount, for 1977, was £5,000. We set off early for that one, Eric hated being late, and we collected Jimmy on the way. I recall this was all filmed for posterity by someone in the charity, but again unfortunately, I have never actually seen it. Jimmy and Eric were clowning around in the back, which spilled out when they arrived. Stood there with the Duke of Edinburgh, tugging the microphone leads, laughing and generally acting exactly the way you're not supposed to in the presence of royalty. But this was Eric Morecambe, a character just like his television persona, and he wasn't about to let this opportunity to make people laugh slip him by.

Eric saw the inside of Buckingham Palace many more times,

whilst I sat there being watched as I scratched my leg deciding what to listen to on the radio. Many drivers had the same dilemma and we often shared our thoughts during the longer periods. I was waiting around with my sandwich, casually listening to Shirley Bassey, when I noticed another driver I had met before.

As a driver you often see the same faces at different events in the way bus drivers recognise each other and occasionally flash their lights or wave. Of course being a professional driver we couldn't do that, but during the waiting process, we would often have chats to help pass the time. This particular driver was Dave, a pool driver for Buckingham Palace, and he would often drive Prince Charles around to his many social events. We both had a few hours to spare and I think he took pity on my cheesy snack.

Dave had a flat overlooking Grosvenor Place, a very posh and select location, which he shared with his wife. The place was not what I expected looking at it from outside. Very basic, but nonetheless, very comfortable, and we enjoyed a very palatable snack whilst swapping stories of our work. Interestingly, well at least for a chauffeur, it turns out that Palace drivers never have to endure the rigorous cleaning after a long journey. Because they hardly ever go outside London, the cars never get covered in mud from country lanes and salt from motorways. They still have to polish them, and make sure everything inside and out is in perfect condition, but that's an easy life!

These small things, the break from normality, are what made my job interesting. Yes I got to meet famous people, but in many ways it's the ordinary working people whose generosity sticks in your mind. In a way that was like Eric. No matter which celebrity he met, he would still enjoy, and sometimes prefer meeting normal people; the bus driver, the cleaner, the postman.

It wasn't long before Dave and I were back behind the wheel, waiting for the tannoy to tell us what to do. Back to the Palace, back to protocol, back to being watched, and back to the laughter that was Eric Morecambe. He did have a serious side, all though not many people got to see it. During another visit to the Palace when there was less congestion in the courtyard, Eric got back into the car, sat down and before I could do anything he said; "Hold on Mike. I just want to savour this moment. It's not every day you meet Her Majesty." It wasn't the beginning of a joke, or the prequel to some comic anecdote, it was said seriously. He was genuinely touched to be invited to the Palace. The moment passed and we quietly left.

As entertainers both he and Ernie received many awards; some stand out more than others but all of them were greatly appreciated and some even came with perks. When they both were awarded the Freedom of the City of London in 1976, it gave them the right to drive sheep across London Bridge. It's a wonder Eric didn't secretly organise this; I know it would have gone through his head as he stood there with the award, a glint in his eye, imagining some accomplice with a herd of sheep preparing to appear. Another 'perk' of this award, although not something to bring up in polite conversation was the privilege to be hung using a silk scarf instead of rope.

Some of these old traditions would make excellent routines, and I'm sure some of them did. Eric used anything he came across, stored it, broke it down, built it back, changed bits of it and eventually it would pop up on a show or ad-lib.

One special award that was treasured by Eric was the Doctor of Literature, received from Princess Alexandra at Lancaster University in 1977. Not only was it from his part of the world, being in Lancaster, but it also meant he wouldn't have to go to school again! He was very proud of his home town, and mentioned it whenever and wherever he could. How many times has Harpenden popped up in a routine?

He had a deep bond with Morecambe though, the place he was born, and I recall vividly his last trip there. I drove him around the streets almost in silence. The town had declined, run down shops and houses everywhere, dirty roads and a feeling of neglect hung in the air. It really upset him to see his home in such a state. It was almost like they were going downhill together. He was very ill at the time and he just stared out at the boarded up shops and tatty pavements.

I knew had he been in good health he would have done something about it. Raised some money, brought attention to it and done everything he could to bring it back to life. Even the great Midland Hotel, the classic art deco building that once stood so proud, and hosted national and international celebrities, was in bad repair. Eric used to go there to meet friends and have a drink of tea, but this visit was so very different. We both walked in and stared at the state of this once beautiful building. So horrified was he at the sight, that he slowly turned around and left in complete silence.

The town is now back on the up and Eric would have been a part of it all I'm sure, and in a way he is. His statue on the promenade has helped greatly; the recently refurbished Midland and the plans to improve the front would have made him once again proud to say he was born there. There are times I feel really sad he can't see it now or take a stroll down the seafront on a warm summers day, mingling with the throngs of returning tourists. His glasses in his pocket, his hat pulled down and with a fake limp, he would just walk and take in the fresh atmosphere of hope. The smile on his face would be brighter than any illuminations; no need for words.

He would have helped where he could, opening shops or appearing at fetes, like he did all over the country; sometimes with unexpected results.

Chapter 12 – It Must Be Fete

Fetes, jamborees, bazaars, call them what you will, but they all involve a large gathering of local people, homemade foods and competitions to see who can grow the largest, or most unusual vegetable. Another thing they have in common, or at least in the seventies, was that they all tried to outdo each other when getting someone special to open them. Usually this would be a local lad made good such as a cricketer or footballer. Occasionally they might even get a television personality. That's a phrase you don't hear much today, 'television personality'. Maybe it's because most of the people on television don't have a personality and believe too much in their own hype!

You might think this strange, but this is the kind of thing that Eric used to love, and would get very excited about. We would set off, not knowing what the day would throw at us, and Eric used to revel in the challenge that no matter what happened, he had to be funny. That was his job. Maybe it was a way of keeping himself on form, seeing what the crowds would say and if he could make a joke out of it, maybe he just wanted to give something back. The public had made him what he was, they watched the shows, they bought the records and came to see the shows. Now, whenever possible, he would give a little back. There was also the possibility of meeting eccentric people; he could use these as characters in some later sketch.

As you can imagine, Eric was a real crowd-puller and if he was to open a fete, you could guarantee large numbers of people would attend. Maybe not so much to eat the local food or gaze in admiration at large vegetables, but definitely to meet and get the autograph of Eric. It was a weird fascination people had with him often causing incidents that would have people rolling around laughing. One of the incidents that stick in my mind happened at Longparish. Previously we had been there to visit Eric's friend Muriel Young, a children's television producer. Whilst there Eric was asked if he would open the local fete to which he agreed immediately.

It was a beautiful sunny day when we arrived and we were ushered into the VIP tent away from the crowds. We would meet the organisers, some of the carefully selected few who were displaying things, told about various things to watch out for (like the large marrow in row three!) and generally given time to acclimatise. The running events of the day were also discussed so we knew where to be and what was happening to make sure we were out of the beer tent in time.

On this day Muriel would start things off with the welcome speech followed by the introduction of Eric and a few notes about important events and start times. As she went through her list, Eric couldn't help but interrupt from time to time, after all, that is what he was there for.

"..and at 2pm the vegetable competition will be judged."

"Oo, we can't forget the vegetables, I've heard there's a whopper in there... I've heard that about you country folk.... what *do* you put on them...? I've got something that could do with that..."

After the opening, the day's events began with various pet competitions followed by music from local schools or clubs, then finally the interval where at last we could get over to the beer tent for a well needed drink and a light snack.

We never had more than the one drink, but we did indulge in the homemade food. Sausage rolls, quiche, sandwiches, pate and cake, who said I didn't get perks. Walking around looking at various bowls and platters, pretending to know what I was looking at. Tasting things, nodding, telling Eric he should try a particular one; I was only there for my lunch! To the cooks though it was very important, there were reputations at stake here and we had to be careful not to upset any of them. We couldn't approach the five times winner of the dessert competition and advise her she needed more sherry in her trifle, even if we thought it.

After the lunch, and when we were absolutely stuffed full of local goodies it was Eric's favourite part; meeting the public. There was usually a small tent or table set up somewhere, which inevitably had the longest queue, sometimes before we even arrived.

"What are they waiting for?"

"You!"

"Oh! They'll have a hell of wait; I'm having my dinner! Shouldn't they be polishing their cucumbers or something?"

Once in place the crowds grew even more. One by one they waited in turn, eager to meet him, trying not to be nervous or forget what they were planning to ask him. As their turn arrived Eric would smile, shake their hand, fire off a few gags, sign something, thank them for coming and turn to the next one. It wasn't a chore, this was Eric meeting his fans, and he would have stayed there all day if time allowed. He would very often overrun his planned time, chatting with people he had something in common with, telling jokes and making people aware that he was human.

Most of the people that came to see Eric at these events were fans, some of who had met him before or who just wanted to see if he was the same off screen as he was on; most, but not all. On one occasion, something quite unexpected happened. A pretty young girl approached Eric at one event, as the stalls were packing up and the crowds were leaving. They exchanged smiles and she handed over an autograph book, which Eric gladly took. He dropped into his routines, one-liners, tilted glasses, the whole thing, and the girl never broke another smile. She just stood there patiently waiting for him to finish writing his name, seemingly immune from his comedy. Had this girl had her funny bone surgically removed? Did she not know who this man was? Eric kept up the jokes, but still not a twinkle. Eventually, a bit confused and now stammering a bit, he handed the book back to the stony-faced girl.

"Ta," she said. "It's for me Mam."

There was a pause.

"I can't stand you myself, but wait till I tell me Mam you're deaf."

Eric's face was a picture, priceless. He backed off a little way, which brought roars of laughter from the remaining people still waiting to meet him. This was one of those moments that no one can predict. The girl left happy with her autograph and a story to tell her mother. People usually say that autographs are for other people, but in this case I think it was genuinely true.

Fetes usually raise money for charities, and Eric was no stranger to that idea. He was involved in many charities, the closest to his heart was the Lord's Taverners, which Joan is still involved with. This wonderful club was started in the 1950s by a group of cricket loving actors, to raise money for various worthy charities, and are still going strong today. They regularly hold charity cricket matches with teams made up of famous cricketers and show business stars. Many a celebrity has walked out on a fine summers day to strike a few balls in aid of a good cause. Names like Bill Maynard, John Alderton, John Cleese, Rod Hull, Barry Cryer, Roy Castle, Jimmy Hill and Terry Wogan all made appearances.

Eric and Ernie would try to attend the matches whenever they could, but a very busy schedule meant that sometimes one or both of them just couldn't manage it. Ernie would play if he could but Eric, due to his health, had to sit and watch from the stand, a cool beer in one hand and his pipe in the other. On one occasion though he actually broke ranks and umpired. Ernie was there too and they turned it into a comedy routine right in front of the crowds. Ernie strode on to the pitch, fully dressed for cricket but with a giant-sized bat. Close behind was Eric, dressed not at all for cricket. He had pencil-thin legs sticking out of his short trousers, a large, ruffled white jacket and two oddly shaped hats on his head. The idea was theirs and it was a joy to be present during these mad moments of inspiration.

That was a one-off and Eric was usually content to sit and watch, knowing full well that his efforts elsewhere made up for this restful time. Eric worked hard. He worked hard for his television shows, he worked hard for his family, he worked hard for charity; it seemed his niche in life was to work hard. That's not to say he resented it, far from it, he found it very fulfilling. After all, once he and Ernie were into the early to mid seventies, they could afford to ease back, but they didn't.

Eric became president of the Lord's Taverners in 1977, taking over the reins from Prince Charles, and remained there for three years. During his stay his money-raising efforts were spectacular, even beating the Prince one year, which he loved to recount at parties. He would, in a nice way, charge for photographs of himself with anyone or anything. Just a small amount, £1 being the minimum, more if he could sweet talk you. There must be thousands of photographs out there of Eric posing with random people in the street, just back from shopping, in a shop, petrol station or pub. I have even seen pictures of Eric with dogs and snakes! It was all for a good cause however and no one ever complained.

When he was on particular good form during a cricket match and a sizable crowd had gathered round him, as is usually the case, there would be more people watching him than the actual game. The crowd and queue contained the full spectrum of people, all there for the same reason. There was no pushing or shoving, just laughter and excitement. Small babies, toddlers and children, wide-eyed and giggling, almost as exciting as going to see Father Christmas. Teenagers and young couples, middle-aged men and women, grannies and granddads all mixed together, brought there by this incredible man. Carpenters, cooks, painters, drivers, authors, politicians and even other celebrities, it still amazes me today. Once EM 100 pulled up, everyone wanted to see Eric. It didn't matter what walk of life they were from, pauper to royalty, they all wanted to see him, incredible.

As a chauffeur I wasn't strictly required within the walls of the ground, but Eric would get me in, knowing how much I love cricket. He would always try to make sure I was involved with these things and as a result I would often meet my sporting heroes, not to mention a few famous people. Once inside it was not just watching the match either. I would have lunch with these people, me, a driver and ex-postman, sat down to lunch with Harry Secombe and Sir John Mills. Chatting with John Price, John Snow, Bill Edrich and Freddie Trueman. Sometimes I had to pinch myself, but made sure no one was watching at the time.

To top things off I actually got to play in one match; well more like participate really, you can't call my efforts 'playing'. It was one of those long summer nights and a well supported match was about to start when they realised that whoever the umpire was had not turned up. Looking around for a substitute they settled on me after turning up blanks everywhere else. Pulling on a long white coat over my chauffeur's uniform, I proudly walked out on to the pitch. Up came the first bowler; one of my heroes, Freddie Trueman. A few bowls in and Freddie caught the batter LBW. I pointed upwards, which in cricketing terms means "out". The other umpire, who I can't recall, shouted "not out" at which point all hell broke loose.

He was obviously out, I was right behind him at the time but the crowd were not too pleased; they wanted more entertainment and to see more fund raising but I had just called 'out'. I quickly changed my decision and shouted "No ball", hoping this would calm things down, it didn't. Freddie took umbrage and stormed towards me. The crowd were loving it as he chased me around the wicket protesting at my call. It was, of course, all in good humour, and we and the crowd had a good laugh.

The match eventually continued and the end result was thousands of pounds going to charity and me having a sore back and legs for 24 hours. But it was worth it; I had actually been on the same pitch as Freddie Trueman. This is one of many such incidents that I considered a perk of my job. If it didn't involved washing, polishing, digging, cleaning or cutting, to me it was a perk. Not all perks were of the nice kind though. Some were downright dangerous, but even so, still managed to raise a smile.

Chapter 13 – Perks and Peril

With fame of course came many outings, events and luncheons. Eric and Ernie, like all other celebrities, got these in abundance. That is not to say I missed out, as Eric's driver I often managed to sneak into events and meet other famous people as mentioned in the previous chapter. Much of the time Eric would do his best to get me in and I have lost count of the free soft drinks I have been given, but there were more than drinks and social events.

Although there was no connection and definitely no friendly persuasion, my favourite football team is Luton Town. I had been a fan long before I met Eric and both my parents and grandparents came from there. Because of Eric's connection with the club, he arranged game passes for me, which I shall remain ever grateful. He didn't have to, I didn't ask him or drop hints, he just did it.

Of course Eric became a Luton fan almost by accident when his son Gary made a blind decision. Eric decided to take Gary to a football match and so we climbed into the car and headed off not knowing our final destination.

"OK Gary," Eric said, as we approached a junction. "Which way, left or right?"

Gary thought for a moment, not knowing where each direction would take us.

"Left," he said.

Turning the car I headed towards Luton and for Eric, a lifelong connection. For anyone wondering, the other direction would have taken us to Watford, the club that Elton John was a director of at the time. I sometimes wonder what would have happened had Gary made a different choice.

Eric of course eventually became a director of Luton in 1970 and remained in that position until 1975, after which he became vice president until he died in 1984. This gave him, and me, access to areas within the ground that the public never got to see. This was so exciting for me as a lifelong fan, and I think Eric knew how much it meant to me. I could see the changing rooms, the showers, the bar and the VIP areas; I was like a child in a sweet shop.

On one such visit, we had watched the game and had moved into the bar for after game drinks. By this time the ground was almost empty and the fans had gone home, leaving just the ground staff, the players and the special guests. The bar was full of well-known faces, I didn't know where to look first; among them, Luton's manager at the time, Harry Haslam. I was in awe of everything, and then the team arrived, fresh from the dressing room and in need of refreshment. Harry though had other ideas and he grabbed one of them and pulled him aside.

The player, a very good player and one of the best at the time, Jimmy Ryan, was dragged out of the bar and back on to the pitch, very much to his surprise. Eric and I were keen to find out what was going on, along with several other players, so we followed.

Emerging from the tunnel into the empty ground, Harry pointed to the pitch.

"OK son," he said, "show me where the hole is."

The player looked at Harry quizzically and didn't know what to say. Glances were exchanged by the people watching who were just as confused.

"Come on," Harry continued, "there's got to be one. Remember the hole?"

Jimmy, and the rest of us were still baffled. Harry waited a few seconds.

"You must do," he continued, "because you were hiding in it for the whole of the second half!"

The player stood there speechless.

Eric was doing his best not to fall over from laughing, grabbing my arm for support as the others all tried to hide their smirks. Harry turned around and marched back into the bar leaving poor Jimmy staring at the pitch. That moment will never leave me for so many different reasons. If it hadn't been for Eric's generosity, I would have never been there and witnessed it. Eric was like that, he accepted me and my family into his, and whenever he could he would share.

Just after the 1976 Christmas show, Elton John who appeared as a guest invited Eric down to Watford to watch a game of football. He was chairman at the time and knew Eric loved the game. As a keen fan he obviously agreed straight away and so we set off on the due date arriving in plenty of time at our hotel. Once unpacked we headed off to meet up with Elton for a bite to eat. There I was, having lunch with Elton John. He was such a lovely man, very quiet and unassuming, completely different from his on-stage persona. We had our lunch and soon found ourselves in the ground enjoying the Watford game. At half time we went inside to the private bar for a drink and was introduced to his mother who he had brought along. Not only a good game of football with great seats but to watch it in the company of Eric and Elton was an amazing experience.

It wasn't just moments or events he shared; he even shared his beautiful home in Harpenden. My wife and I would often house-sit for him when he visited his villa in Portugal. That in itself was a huge perk. Sitting there in luxury, well-kept garden (I put a lot of work into it!), well-kept house, (I did some work in there too!), well-kept pool (me again!) and a raft of luxury cars (yes, you get the picture!).

When Eric attended a luncheon and I hadn't got my cheese sandwich, he would often get me a seat. Not in the kitchen, or tucked away in a corner, but a seat at his table, next to him. I sometimes think the other guests were too polite to ask who I was and assumed I was some new celebrity. Sometimes I felt like one, much to my embarrassment and Eric's joy. It was a small luncheon for a charity, which has long since left my memory, but I was sat next to Eric. As we ate I noticed a member of the public heading towards our table; I could almost feel Eric searching for his pen and his mind working on a joke. The lady smiled as she looked at each person on the table in turn before settling on me.

"Excuse me, could I have your autograph?" she said, handing me something to write on.

You can imagine the look on the other guests' faces, Eric in particular was a mix of astonishment and hysterics, another priceless moment. One to me I thought, but several thousand to Eric. The lady left unaware of whose autograph she had just got and whose she had failed to get. I wonder if she was sent over by someone else; told to get Eric's autograph but didn't know which one he was.

A part of any celebrity life nowadays of course, is advertising; it generates a lot of income for the star or stars involved, and Eric and Ernie were no different. In their early BBC years it was difficult to do because of strict BBC rules. They couldn't do television adverts until much later when they moved to commercial television, but that didn't stop them putting their names to a host of other things.

There are many, many companies and products that Eric, Ernie or both of them advertised, ranging from computer games, bread, cars, paint, petrol and even lager. With this came freebies, some of which found their way to me, not because they didn't like the product, but because they just got too much of it! How was anyone able to go through hundreds of loaves of bread in a year?

For Eric, it was all just a bit of fun, although they did pick and choose what to advertise. They had plenty of offers, but they chose only to do certain ones. Take Sunblest bread for example. Eric and Ernie did photo shoots and radio commercials, and even appeared on every loaf of Sunblest bread for a time. Offering jokes to bring a bit of sunshine to the start of your day. These commercials worked and brought in huge amounts of money for the company, even Eric was amazed at how sales jumped up just because he and Ernie were involved. Advertising Sunblest earned Eric a huge, regular shipment of the product, which was mirrored by other companies who he worked with. If it worked with bread or paint, it was no surprise that Eric jumped at the chance to be involved with cars, in particular Saab.

Saab at the time were trying to rival Ford and Vauxhall but went about it in a different, but clever way. Instead of using Eric and Ern to promote their products to the public, they used them at corporate events within the company. The boys, either together or individually, would turn up at employee meetings or company briefings to help motivate staff and executives and give important corporate customers a boost. This was done in a way to fit in with their workload, and as part of that they had to make video and audio recordings as well as turning up in person.

It was fun, but as Eric correctly said, it was still work. They still expected him to be funny, and he couldn't let them down. But he did get the perks. As part of Saab's strategy, which again proved very innovative, Eric and Ern were each given a new Saab car complete with tax disc. They could use the cars for whatever they wanted, wherever they wanted. What this did was allow Morecambe and Wise to be seen in Saab's cars, thus giving them free advertising every time Eric or Ern went out. What could be a greater advert – actually seeing the stars using the products? Saab also knew that Eric and Ern would always go to the best areas, again advertising the product to the audience that Saab were looking to get into. Some executive was having a good day when he thought of that idea.

Because of the large scale of motoring companies, they often held large public events to promote a new model or initiative and Saab were no different. Usually held in London these events would either be inside a large hall, so people could see the cars close up, or outside when people could see the cars in action. They would follow the usual plan of food, cars, music, cars, raffle, cars, awards… you get the idea; promotion, promotion, promotion.

At one particular event I recall getting a rather nice, but at the same time worrying surprise. The event consisted of all the usual things and the first prize of the raffle was a holiday weekend abroad. Everyone took part and Eric was asked to make the draw. Quite unexpectedly, I was asked to help him draw the runners-up prizes; second best again! So there we both were, on stage together, it was magic and nerve-racking all at the same time. You never knew what Eric would say or do in these circumstances, it was all off the cuff with no script. Stood there facing even a small crowd made me appreciate Ernie's role even more, only I was onstage with Eric Morecambe.

He was on form as usual, firing off volley after volley of one-liners and gags, the audience loved it. Luckily I was not needed other than to stand there looking on, trying not to get noticed. Then came the draw and Eric pulled out the winning ticket – making jokes and comments with and about each winner as they collected their prize. Eventually we got to the fourth prize, a lovely crystal decanter and glasses. Because we were taking it in turn to pull out the winners, Eric dipped his hand into the bag and pulled out a number. He read it out but there was not the usual cheer from the audience. All the tickets had been sold but no one was owning up to winning this prize. Everyone was looking around for the winner, but still no one claimed it. It was all a mystery, except to me; Eric had pulled out my number.

I had bought a ticket in the spirit of the occasion, but was far too embarrassed now to step forward and claim the prize. Surely everyone would think it was a fix. It wasn't until later in the evening that a Saab employee told me to go and claim it. "After all," he said, "Why buy a ticket?" The answer of course, was because I felt I had to, but now I had actually won and didn't know what to do. I did finally get the courage to collect my prize, and still have it to this day. Despite many house moves it is still in perfect condition and a lovely reminder of a great, if not slightly embarrassing day. It is just one of many items which hold fond memories.

Another Saab event I attended has left me with memories of sheer terror. It was an employees only open day at Silverstone, the famous racetrack. Eric was duly invited and agreed to turn up. Despite having a Saab, he wanted to go in the Rolls, so I prepared the car and we set off. From Eric's face in the rear mirror, I could tell he was excited about this one. There are some places that affect you, I suppose it goes back to when we were children and watched excitedly as race cars roared around a track on television. With Eric smiling all of the way, we made our way to the circuit.

Luckily we arrived just in time for lunch, and we were both seated in the large marquee and suitably fed. Again, Eric got me at his table, this time surrounded by various Saab managers. Turning around I suddenly realised that sat next to me was not a suited Saab employee but Barbara Dickson, the singer. What a bizarre feeling, sandwiched between Eric Morecambe and Barbara Dickson.

After our food a Saab representative had arranged for us to take a tour of Silverstone. Upon hearing this, the schoolboy in both of us took over and we were suddenly excited young men eager to see the sights and experience the race atmosphere. It was no longer famous celebrity and driver but two smiling and giggling adolescents. We were even going to be driven around the circuit; this was getting better by the minute. What they didn't tell us, or at least tell us until we were getting into the cars, was that we were to be driven around the circuit by Erik Carlsson.

For those too young to remember, Erik was a famous rally driver, driving for Saab, from the fifties through to the seventies. Because of his work on and off the track, he was called Mr. Saab. He even helped out on Bond films.

As Eric climbed into the car, with me close behind, something suddenly dawned on him. Maybe it was the helmets, maybe it was the harness that strapped us in, maybe it was the roll cage but this wasn't going to be a gentle guided tour. His face turned from excitement to anxiety in a second as he looked around the car and wondered what the hell was going to happen. I guess I had a similar look too; I was scared stiff and was grabbing hold of anything I could.

Once we were strapped in and the safety checks done, Erik started the car, paused for a split second and then hammered the accelerator down. The car and its contents shot off like a rocket, forcing my head back into the seat. Eric was in the front so I have no idea what was going through his mind or what expression he had; I was too busy trying to stay alive. I was in the back so didn't get a clear view of the track, which is probably for the best really. The engine roared as Erik threw the car into the corners, tyres screeching underneath us. After the third or fourth bend I had got used to it and was grinning like a Cheshire cat. Luckily because of the vibrations, no one could tell I was shaking like a leaf as well.

As each corner approached we braced ourselves and let the adrenalin rush through our bodies. The car lurched and twisted under the expert control of Erik, smoke pouring from the wheels as we glided sideways around another corner. As the finish line approached Erik slammed on the brakes and brought the car to an abrupt, sliding stop, flinging us about like rag dolls. It's a good job we were strapped in or we both would have ended up on the tarmac.

As we both climbed out, still shaking, we still had those silly smiles on our faces. Eric came round from the other side to compare them and to see how much I was shaking; I think it was a draw. Erik clambered out and joined us, knowing full well he had just scared the living daylights out of us!

"I wasn't trying to push the car today," he said, smiling, "it really wasn't up to scratch."

"Thank God for that!" Eric quipped through twitching lips.

As we walked back to the tables, both still quivering, Eric looked at me and grinned.

"I'm glad I wore brown trousers today."

The rest of the day went well, despite our now aching muscles, and soon it was time for us to leave. We said our goodbyes and Eric this time sat in the front seat of the Rolls. I sat down in the driver's seat, closed the door and looked over at him, my foot hovering over the accelerator.

"Don't even think about it sunshine!"

It was a step too far I think, and even though we both thoroughly enjoyed our ride, we both preferred more gentle sports. I slowly drove off, much to the relief of Eric and my aching body.

Of course it could be considered a perk just to be able to drive a Rolls Royce, but what about when you can use it for yourself? As generous as Eric was, what he did for me on 14th March 1982 will always stand out in my mind. It not only affected me, but also a certain lady who I had met a few years earlier.

Chapter 14 – A Special Day

In 1980 I was single and living with friends Bob and Sheila in Luton. I was working for Eric but this still left me with some spare time. Bob was working as a jobbing builder and was a bit fed up with work and was looking to move on. We talked about doing something together on the understanding that my driving duties would still be priority. Eventually we settled on the idea of opening a shop and quickly began looking for suitable premises. A few weeks later and we had settled for a nice little place on Farley Hill in Luton.

The shop had accommodation above it, which was an added bonus and meant I could get out from under my friends feet. Bob would take on the shop full-time, and I would help out whenever Eric didn't need me.

We took on the cleaner, Vi Chapman, from the previous owners, and she was kept busy two or three times a week keeping things in tip-top condition. As we chatted one day she mentioned that her daughter was due back from holiday and that I should meet her. I nodded and thought no more about it. Several weeks went by and there was no further mention of her daughter so I presumed whatever plans she had were either forgotten or put on hold.

Another week passed and again we were chatting in the shop when a girl walked past the window. She must have caught my attention because unknown to me, I was staring at her, or as Vi claimed, ogling. Vi continued chatting and I continued staring, not hearing a thing she said until I felt a sharp pain in my ribs.

"Oi!" Vi said, her elbow poised to strike again, "Watch it. That's my daughter you're looking at. That's my Lesley."

Lesley duly came into the shop and I can't say it was love at first sight because I think true love comes from getting to know somebody and growing in life together, but it was pretty damn close. We were introduced and somehow through my drooling and staring I managed to get a date with her. This, I thought to myself, must be the most romantic date ever, so powerful and beautiful that she can't help but fall in love with me. I took her to the cash and carry warehouse at Sundon Park in Luton and we touched hands on a shopping trolley. Maybe not the ideal first date, but isn't it a lovely feeling when your heart flutters and you feel all warm inside.

It didn't put us off though and thereafter we went out together whenever we could. Eventually I did the right thing and we got married at Luton registry office on 14th March 1981. A special day for more than one reason, it was also Lesley's birthday and she had just got me as a present.

Our limousine for this very special occasion was my dad's two-door Hillman Imp. Not a shining white Rolls Royce, or even Eric's Rolls Royce, but that didn't matter to us. Dad made a very good chauffeur for the day and for once I was in the back.

We had our reception at Farley Hill Primary School and the food was prepared and served by family and friends, most of it was bought from the cash and carry where we had our first date – how romantic. Sadly Eric was out of the country on holiday at the time, which meant he couldn't attend, but nothing could distract from the great day. And I knew he wished us well.

The early days of our marriage were fraught for Lesley. I was recovering from my slight heart attack, which is covered in an earlier chapter, and at the same time had the most horrendous experience that she had to keep from me until I was in a good enough condition.

My operation was planned and I was in hospital waiting for the all-clear, which was due any hour. Back home and my stepmother

Amy and my father were staying with us, to lend a hand during my recuperation. Lesley was just finishing off some ironing and clearly recalls she had two shirts left to do. It's funny how these things stick in your mind.

"I'm just going over the road." She said, meaning that she was just going to see her own parents that lived, funnily enough, across the road.

"I'll finish those off for you." Amy had said.

"No, it doesn't matter," Lesley insisted, "but let me know when you've finished."

Laughing, Lesley left to visit her parents to keep them informed about my operation. She was gone only five minutes, and was walking back home when she noticed my father on the balcony of the maisonette. She assumed he was taking some air or just waiting to see her come back, but when she got to him his face was white as a sheet.

"She's gone." He said.

"Where?" Lesley asked, thinking Amy had gone for a walk.

"No – she's gone."

Amy had laid down on the settee and passed away in the five minutes that Lesley was out. Lesley was in shock and didn't know what to do, my father was in a terrible state and there I was, miles away in a hospital waiting to have a life-saving operation.

Lesley's father took control of things, he was used to this kind of incident as he had worked for an undertakers. He quickly called for an ambulance and calmed everyone down. Now they had to make a decision – should they tell me?

Lesley contacted the surgeon, Professor Yacoub and asked his advice. He understood the situation but advised her not to tell me. I had to stay in hospital, I had to have the operation, and any stress could have an adverse effect. Reluctantly she took his advice, keeping that information away from me. She must have been an emotional wreck, I don't know how she managed, but she pulled through with the strong support of her family and especially her mother Vi. She eventually told me three days later, a huge release of pressure and emotion.

One year later and our first anniversary was quickly approaching and I was hoping Eric didn't require my services. I was planning a nice meal out with Lesley and was praying my car duties would not get in the way. Planning anything was hard when you were a chauffeur as you could be called upon at any time of the day or night. I had risked it, and had planned as far as I dared ahead, eight hours! That was in the evening though and as usual I still had my car and caretaking duties to perform during the day.

This particular day I had been poking about in the flower beds pretending I knew the difference between flowers and weeds. Eric appeared at the door of his house, looked around and strolled slowly across to me. Would this just be a little chat about the weather or fishing? I quickly checked the pile of weeds, searching for anything that looked flower-like in case I had dug up something that Eric had planted previously. Nothing.

"Michael," he said, he always called me by my full name, "Could you make sure the Rolls is ready. I need it for this evening. Thanks."

Needing the car meant that he needed a driver too, which had blown my anniversary plans in the air. My heart sank and my shoulders must have dropped. My face changed, although I tried to hide my disappointment, but he picked up on it straight away.

"Is there a problem?" he enquired.

It wasn't a question asked by an employer, or by someone who expects his driver to obey, it was a question asked by a friend who was concerned and recognised that something had not gone to plan. I told him that it was my wedding anniversary and of my plan to take Lesley out for an evening meal. After a short thought, he smiled.

"That's not a problem," he said, "bring her along."

This was Eric Morecambe. It was 1982 and Morecambe and Wise were on top of their game and probably the most famous television personalities in the UK. Many stars change with fame, they look down on others because of their position, but not Eric. He was still down to earth, the nicest man you're likely to meet, a compassionate man who tried to look after everyone from royalty to the ordinary man in the street and the man currently on his hands and knees surrounded by what he hoped were weeds. He treated all of them exactly the same and you always came away with a wonderful warm feeling afterwards.

I called Lesley at work and told her to be ready for collection; I would be picking her up in the Rolls. Not only that, but Eric would be there as well for the early part of the evening. You can imagine how she felt. Being taken out for a meal with me... well, maybe it was the fact that it would be in the Rolls with Eric Morecambe. Whatever the real reason, she was extremely excited and had told everyone at work. I don't know which part she was looking forward to most, but I confidently hoped it was the meal.

She had met Eric many times before of course, and was always charmed by him, and enjoyed his company immensely. But this was a little different, this time she would be in the Rolls, being chauffeured around London, this was her night. I think she completely forgot that I would actually be working!

Six thirty and I was picking up Eric from his home in Harpenden. As he climbed in, he leant over and slipped a ten-pound note into my hand.

"A small something to help with the anniversary," he smiled.

Remember this was 1982 and ten pounds was worth a whole lot more. Was this out of guilt? Was he showing off his wealth? Definitely not. It was Eric being Eric. Thinking of others and showing how thoughtful and kind he was. He didn't have to do that, he certainly didn't do it out of any sense of duty. He was just a naturally nice person. He knew what it meant to have a wedding anniversary and he knew I was being put out by driving him. Nevertheless, it was a gesture of friendship that I will never forget. Remember also that he allowed me to use his car, his Rolls Royce, for my own personal benefit that night. A true gent.

We drove to a sporting dinner in London that was to be teeming with sports personalities. With Lesley in the back, we arrived at the same time as Dickie Davies, and being close friends with Eric, he soon joined us for a chat. Lesley had suffered a miscarriage earlier in the year and it was obvious that Eric had fed this, and our anniversary details to him. Dickie gave Lesley a hug. He was a lovely warm and genuine man, which came across straight away. Eric and he kindly congratulated us both on our anniversary before heading inside, leaving Lesley and myself to enjoy our evening. Lesley was now glowing with excitement; this night had been made so special for her. I did get the feeling though, that I was rapidly moving down the list of favourites.

Lesley had not seen very much of London, so I took her for a quick tour of the major sights. Buckingham Palace, Trafalgar Square, the Houses of Parliament, Soho... well maybe not there. This must have been magical for her. Seeing things from inside such a special car always made a huge difference and added to the night, even though I was still driving!

We eventually found a place to eat; a fish and chip restaurant in Endell Street. The only one I knew of that did a good steamed fish. I had tried many others, but this one was head and shoulders above the rest, you could tell that by the sheer number of taxis parked up outside. It was always busy, and a favourite of mine. After the meal we took a slow walk along the side of the Thames before heading back to that car so we could pick up Eric.

That was a night Lesley and I will never forget even though I was working. I guess I was at the bottom of the 'it was a very special night because…' list, but it was still a memorable and unique occasion for the both of us.

Rehearsal room during the Thames years (1980) with John Ammonds, Hugh Paddick and Hannah Gordon

Me sat in Eric's bath with my son helping out

Eric prepares for the Knorr corporate film

The Queen at the statue unveiling in 1999

The 1971 Rolls Royce during its renovation by Peter Yates

Eric (the statue) waves to Eric (the car)

Peter, me and the finished Rolls in 2012

With Eric's wife Joan in 2012

Reacquainted with Charlie – 2012

The Jensen Interceptor during renovation

The Morecambe & Wise bus

Me, Richard and Julie Want, Neil and Janine Martin – Brief encounter with Eric

My grandson – starting early

Always with me…

Chapter 15 – The Fisherman

It was no secret that Eric loved fishing, he even wrote a book about it, *Eric Morecambe On Fishing*, which he finished a few months before his death. Fishing, probably more than other sports, has by design plenty of room for tall stories and fascinating adventures. Clambering through the undergrowth in search of that elusive trout; sitting for hours beneath a flimsy tent in torrential rain and of course the one that got away. It's a relaxing sport that lets the brain meander as much as the river, probably the reason for such exaggerated tales of missed opportunities.

In Eric's case, it was this very fact that drew him so much. His brain was constantly active, coming up with new jokes, firing off one-liners and keeping up his comic persona every second of every day. Fishing enabled him to relax and get away from it all by having to sit, or stand, quietly for hours on end, with no one else around. He mostly went fishing alone, but when he preferred company, it was from a very small collection of close friends who he could relax with, one being Dickie Davies. You were very privileged indeed if you ever got your feet wet with Eric.

Fishing was in his blood. His grandfather was a fisherman in Morecambe and his father caught fish to supplement his meagre wages working for the council. On these trips his father sometimes took Eric along, probably to try and keep him out of trouble. Eric caught the bug and it soon became his passion. It helped him to slow down, to clear his head and to be alone in his otherwise hectic life.

Ernie found different ways to relax, taking his motor launch up the Thames or flying out to his villa in Florida, but Eric sought sanctuary alone. There was no better relaxation for him than by the river with just nature for company. The twitter of birds, the scurrying of voles and the gentle hiss of the water, his own little bit of paradise right here in England.

It wasn't his only way to relax however, he also had a villa in Portugal that he regularly visited when filming allowed. He wasn't a beach man, preferring to sit in the shade and write, or think of ideas for shows. He also loved birdwatching; strolling through the countryside, binoculars in hand; again it was a solitary hobby close to nature. Fishing though was still king and whenever he had time and the weather was right, the gear would be packed up and plans made.

He immersed himself into it like any other keen fisherman. He had to know every aspect, every detail, whether it was about bait, rods, flies or the fish themselves. He even learned how to make his own flies; a very skilled and time-consuming job that required patience and dexterity. But the finished items would be displayed with pride on his favourite fishing hat, ready to be used should the correct criteria be met. Of the very few people who did go fly fishing with him, they all say he could cast a good fly. I suppose that was Eric's character coming through, his constant, striving to be the best he could be. Whatever he did, it had to be to the best of his ability.

I could usually tell when a good fishing day was about to begin. Maybe it was the weather, maybe knowing there was some spare time to waste or the glance from Eric as he surveyed the clouds.

"Pack the car Michael." He would say with a smile, "We're going fishing."

Some of the time I had already packed it; you just knew when things were right. With the car full, we would disappear off to one of a few preferred sites, the river Kennet in Kentbury was always a favourite.

Depending on conditions, how much time he had, and of course the weather, his fishing trips would last between a single day, to over a week. I would drop him off and leave him alone until a prearranged time. Sometimes this meant me driving off to a local pub for a few hours, going back home or just parking up in a lay-by and having a cheese sandwich. For the longer trips I would go back home. You can't really stay in a lay-by for a week can you, the cheese would go stale and you would probably be arrested.

The collection time was exact, and that was not to be ignored. If I arrived a little early I had to wait. Eric would see me but continue fishing until the time he had specified, no longer, no sooner. If, heaven forbid, I was late, no excuse would wash, which is why I was never late. I never tried my luck and as a professional driver, always took account of road conditions, traffic, time of day etc. Much better to be early, enjoy a sandwich and some Shirley Bassey than to be late.

Like all fishermen the world over, he didn't catch a fish every time, but this didn't bother him. The fact he was away from it all, surrounded by nature and fully relaxed doing something he enjoyed was most important. A fish on the line would be the icing on the cake though, and kind of closure to the days events and something to brag about to anyone who cared to listen.

Because of the randomness of the sport, you could never tell if the fish were biting so it would be a mistake to anticipate these things. Eric once did though, and the fact that it all went wrong caused him to take alternative action. He had promised Joan he would return with a large catch for the family and duly set off full of confidence. The weather was just right, he had the time and he was looking forward to a nice day's fishing. I dropped him off and watched as he picked his way to the river. He surveyed the banks, looked at the clouds, felt the wind and then moved into a spot he calculated would give best results. With him settled I turned around and headed off to find a pub.

I had a nice quiet day, reading the newspaper, watching people come in and out and generally relaxing. Eventually though it was time to return to the river and collect him. I finished my drink and climbed back into the Rolls. As soon as I pulled up and caught sight of Eric's face I knew his day hadn't gone well. As we packed the gear into the car it became apparent that despite all of his confidence and promises, he hadn't caught a single thing.

Normally this wouldn't have fazed him, but the fact that he had made a promise to his wife, he was annoyed and I think a little disappointed in himself. The funny thing was, the family didn't even like fresh fish and always gave it away to neighbours; but this didn't matter, a promise was a promise. He had gone there with every intention to at least catch a few, to return triumphant having provided for his family. The fish though had other ideas and didn't even offer so much as a nibble.

What to do? Tell the truth of course.

He had a huge catch, 3 or 4 trout, each weighing at least three pounds. Sadly he had been mugged on the riverbank by a local fish thief who had stolen the lot. Maybe that wouldn't work; how about he made a huge catch but had to throw them back, after all they all had families and children and who was he to split them up. Nothing seemed to work properly and we were getting closer to home. As we passed through a nice little village, he was still trying to find the best solution; honesty was the best policy. No need to make up lies.

"Can you just stop here a moment Michael." He suddenly said with a strange look on his face.

Confused, I pulled over in the village and wondered what he was doing.

Eric opened the door, climbed out and walked straight into a fishmonger's. Several minutes later he emerged holding three large brown trout and beaming from ear to ear. By his smile you would have thought he had caught them himself. I smiled back, a knowing smile, as he climbed back in and closed the door. Chuckling to myself I glanced in the mirror at the man in the back, cradling his catch.

"Shurrup!" he said. "Now let's get home."

When we arrived no one was any the wiser. Eric had kept his promise; he had returned with a nice catch and the fishmonger had sold his fish. After all, Eric didn't actually say he would bring back fish he had caught. The thing was, the trout went straight into the freezer and were given away to neighbours a few days later. Buying fish wasn't a habit he had, in fact this was the only time he did this, well this and the time he entered a fishing competition for charity.

Of all the things that could get Eric involved, fishing, Morecambe and charity were top of the list; put them together and you'd be almost guaranteed to get him there. It was a fishing competition for charity in which he would be representing Morecambe; he couldn't wait. We turned up and set up the gear on his allotted site, set the bait and cast. All day he sat there staring at a float, and caught absolutely nothing. There was no reason in particular; it was just an off day. Under the circumstances he did the only thing he could, cheat. After all, it was for charity and it was for Morecambe.

He didn't want to look bad or let down his home town, so something needed to be done. I have no idea how he did it or where they came from, but one by one he started to land fish. On closer inspection it turned out he was not actually 'catching' them. Where he got them is still a mystery, maybe he brought them with him, maybe the fishmonger had another busy day! Whatever way he did it, he had somehow managed to smuggle in several of them about his person.

His plan was simple. Occasionally he would reel in the line, attach a fish and casually throw it back in. Waiting a few moments he would feign a bite and pull in the dead fish. Brilliant, if no one had been watching. Unluckily, the match marshal had caught sight of his shenanigans and had been watching him for some time, no doubt with a smile on his face. Eric was instantly disqualified, but made the best out of it, and was forgiven by the crowd of laughing onlookers. Forgiveness was not always what he got though.

On his frequent returns to Morecambe, he would try to go fishing back at his boyhood haunts. His destination though had gained a new inhabitant since he was last there, a man called Lionel. Lionel was a Morecambe man who practically lived in the countryside. He had no time for television and other modern distractions, preferring a good book or where possible, a long walk. He disliked noise, people and people making noise.

On one particular day Lionel was sat in the garden of his little cottage watching the world roll by with his trusty dog by his side. The river babbled close by and everything was well with the world. He decided to go for a little walk down by the river to pass a few hours and with his dog, set off across the fields. As he approached, he spotted a man who appeared at first glance to be fishing. He was surrounded by the usual plethora of equipment, rods, flasks, boxes and bait. As he got closer though, he noticed the man was clambering about near the water's edge, thrashing about with a stick. Slapping the water like a madman and rushing around generally being a nuisance. Lionel wasn't having any of this kind of behaviour, and so he set off towards him.

Intent on stopping this maniac from ruining his beloved riverbank and countryside, he marched faster towards this bespectacled man; otherwise known to you and me as Eric Morecambe. Lionel had no idea who it was, he just wanted him to go away and leave the countryside in peace.

"Ay up. What ye doing man? Bloody hell." He shouted, as he got closer.

Eric, for the first time, noticed him and climbed back up the bank.

"Hello there." He said, expecting to be recognised and asked for an autograph.

"Who do ya think ya are," Lionel scolded, "bashing about the place? I bet yer not from round 'er are ye?"

"Don't you recognise me?" Eric asked slightly nervously.

"I haven't the slightest idea."

"I'm Eric Morecambe. I'm on the television."

"Haven't got one." Lionel replied, cutting Eric down to size, "Any road, don't ye go destroying the countryside man. You're all the same ye southerners. Come up 'er bashing about, think you can do what ye likes…"

The one-way conversion went on for a while, and has now drifted into folklore around Morecambe. Local man without television in dressing-down argument with television superstar he didn't know. I wish I had been early that day, or better still had a camera. It's not every day you meet someone who didn't recognise Eric, especially in the seventies. It was one of those fishing trips that didn't go to plan. He went there expecting to be alone, to relax and have a quiet few hours. He did this sometimes just prior to a big event, to recharge and prepare so on the day he would be at his blistering best.

Often it would be big shows, live performances or important events, but sometimes it would be something much closer home; his daughter's wedding is one such example. When for once he didn't want the spotlight; after all, he wasn't the one who was getting married.

Chapter 16 – Sons and Daughters

Sons, daughters, dogs and royalty; that's not a bad name for a book, but it describes my driving role quite well. As mentioned earlier, not only were my talents used for the rich and famous, but also the family. When Gail, Gary and Steven, Eric's children, were at school I was the school-run king. Not content with having three children, they each had their own schools too. I had to organise the timings so that each one wasn't late, and make sure they got to their destination safely.

For this the Rolls would be out of the question so I opted for the trusty old Volvo. A nice, safe car that didn't stand out or draw attention to its occupants. The last thing any child needed was to have their friends poke fun at them for turning up at school each day in a Rolls Royce. In fact Gail disliked her dad being famous so much, she told the teachers and her friends that she was adopted. That was something that later backfired when her mother was questioned about it at a parents' evening.

The Volvo was also spacious, something which was to my benefit when they later went to boarding schools. We turned up with all the clothes and equipment in the large boot while others, more desperate to show off their wealth, struggled with tiny sports cars. Things crammed behind seats, boots tied down with rope, children doubled up somewhere amongst the suitcase and personal belongings. Just to show off their nice, expensive cars. I know which I preferred.

Driving for the family continued until each child moved out and found their own way in life. We didn't lose touch however and were reacquainted many more times for family gatherings at events like Eric and Ernie's O.B.E.

The most memorable, if not the most special event would probably be Gail's wedding in 1975, where not only was I a guest, but also a driver. As an extra incentive, I was told I could not actually join in the ceremony until all of the people had arrived safely. This meant I had to get them all there before I could enjoy this momentous occasion of Eric's daughter getting hitched, something I could not do alone. The wedding day itself, as all weddings are, was a massive exercise in coordination, especially so because of who it was. I knew I was to control the transport and this would mean having additional help. Who could I trust with this important job? The man who was responsible for it in the first place, my old friend from chapter two, Charlie. He gladly agreed, and the old team were back together again, at least for the day.

Gail had known her husband-to-be, Paul, for a long time prior to the wedding and they had enjoyed many a holiday together, even going on an expedition to Africa with a few Land Rovers and what they could carry in bags. Back from her travels and settled down, it was now time to get married. Nerves were jangling in the house as everyone rushed about, staring into mirrors, scrutinising each other's clothes, dusting each other off and looking for dropped pins that held the flowers in place. Yes, your normal, run-of-the-mill chaos that ensues just before the big event; Eric's family were no different.

Eric himself was quite calm; or at least I could not identify anything that showed externally, and I had seen him nervous. He had planned the event in his mind and calmly made sure things were running as smoothly as they could under the circumstances. He had written his speech well in advance, littered with his usual comedic brilliance, and knew it word for word. His most difficult job was trying to play the whole event down to the national press.

This was Gail's day, not his, and he did not want to steal the spotlight from his daughter. As time moved on people began to move quicker; combing hair, adjusting waistcoats, giving shoes a last minute polish, until finally there was nothing left to do but leave the house and get into the waiting cars. Outside I had given the cars an extra polish and with everyone present and correct, still with a few nerves, I got them into their seats.

Charlie was gone by this point; using the Austin Princess he was busy ferrying family and friends while I had the very important job of getting the bridesmaids, Joan and Eric to the church. With the brilliant sunshine, the car sparkled as we made our way to the local parish church in Harpenden.

I knew the wedding was big news locally, but as we approached and turned the bend I could not believe what I saw. I think Eric and the rest of the passengers were a bit shocked too. This was in the days before mobile phones, so no one could have warned us, and by the same logic, no one could contact other people quickly. So where all these onlookers came from is beyond me. Despite Eric's best efforts to play it down, the whole place was packed. Guests mingled with onlookers and well-wishers, newspaper photographers bustled with non-invited guests and the whole scene was like Beatlemania all over again.

Harpenden was a relatively small place but news had travelled fast and journalists from all over the place had appeared. Sadly they were not just there for Gail, who's big day it was, but mainly for Eric. Ernie was also present along with other well-known celebrities, and Des O'Connor (sorry Des, just a little joke in the old tradition). Eric often joked that Des came to the wedding, even though he wasn't invited, but this was all friendly banter. They were very good friends and the fact that Des was there actually proved it. He had flown in from America and came straight from the airport just so he could be with them on this special day.

Other well-known people, all of whom knew Eric away from show business, included Harry Worth, Roy Castle, Harry Secombe and their respective wives and Eric and Ernie's writer Eddie Braben.

The wedding itself went off without a hitch and Charlie and I were soon back on duty, getting people to the reception at St. Michael's Manor Hotel in St. Albans. Again I was under instruction that until every guest had made it there, I could not join the reception, so Charlie and I made sure we got things done pretty quickly.

Sadly, as much as I enjoyed the whole day, I was one of the few who could not drink. I had duties to be carried out, and as all around me slowly emptied bottles of champagne, I stuck to orange juice.

All in the life of a chauffeur.

Chapter 17 – Moving On

As the seventies rolled on towards the eighties, Eric and Ernie again seemed to get that strange itch to do something different. It happened when they were at ATV and now it was happening again. Despite doing three mediocre films in the sixties, they felt they still hadn't reached their full potential on the big screen. Secretly they had also been offered five times their current pay by rival organisation Thames.

The BBC, at that time, had no facilities to make such films and Eric and Ernie's contracts were coming up for renewal. The commercial channel Thames on the other hand, had all of the facilities; they had Euston Films as a subsidiary and could offer not only the films Eric and Ernie wanted, but a whole stack of cash too. All they did was make them an offer they couldn't refuse. In a flourish of newspaper front pages, Morecambe and Wise switched channels in June 1978, leaving the head of the BBC, Sir Bill Cotton, more than a little bemused and upset. It later transpired that Sir Bill had offered to match the money, but could not offer opportunities for films, and was too late to stop the move.

Eric cherished the thought of something new and was looking forward not only to the promised film, but the new challenges of working with different people in a different location. Because Eddie Braben was still under contract at the BBC, Thames now had the almost impossible job of finding new writers. The answer came in the guise of seasoned professionals like John Junkin and Barry Cryer, who although could not match Eddie's experience and connection with the boys, did their very best under the circumstances.

The Thames shows also had to be written differently to take adverts into account. Because of this the shows lost a lot of the natural flow the BBC ones had, and gave an impression of a lot of small bits thrown together, rather than a planned, end to end production.

Time at Thames was not all bad though, as they finally got to fulfil one of their invitations from some old friends. In 1976, on the Morecambe and Wise Show, stars of The Sweeney, John Thaw and Dennis Waterman were special guests. After the filming, John suggested that Eric and Ernie, in return, should come on to The Sweeney. Despite wanting to, the strict BBC rules meant they couldn't do work for a commercial station, and so it appeared it would never happen.

With the move to Thames though, it was all now back on, and a special episode was written for them in 1978. The filming took place at a vehicle testing station near Camberley, with additional work being done at both the Lakeside Club, Frimley, and the studio. It was quite nervous driving to the set, we didn't know what to expect, but we needn't have worried, everyone was so friendly, especially John and Dennis. It turned out that they were especially pleased because it was the first time they had got somewhere nice to change instead of a shed or local public toilet. Because Eric and Ernie were there, the company had supplied caravans. In-between scenes there was always a lot of hanging about, this was filled with a lot of laughter, John and Dennis were really nice people to work with considering their on-screen characters.

During filming we also had to drive to an army training range near Thorpe Park for a week to shoot the outside sequences, and Eric really enjoyed this move away from his normal work. He got to do things that he felt were closer to a movie than a cop show. At one point he was tied to the back of a van full of fish. Not as some kind of torture, but to stop him falling out while the van drove in a mock chase scene. This was only used for close-up shots, Eric being replaced by a stuntman for the more distant, faster shots. Being stood knee-deep in fish didn't seem to worry him at first, that was until the smell refused to leave him after the scene was complete. For days after he stank of fish, we had to drive the Rolls with the windows down to get rid of it. It was like being back in Brighton again!

For a few days the filming moved indoors into the Lakeside club. The scenes mainly revolved around Eric and Ernie doing their ventriloquist act and the villains using the doll as a hiding place for drugs. Because of the scenes, Eric was worried that Charlie, the doll, might get damaged, and being an integral part of their live act, it would spell trouble if this were to happen. Because of this Eric commissioned another doll, identical to the first, just to be used on The Sweeney.

The whole experience was wonderful, working on a top-rated television show with great actors and even getting to watch Eric covered in fish. The catering, I recall, was very good too, another surprise for us, and much better than the BBC canteen. A converted double-decker bus was filled with tables and chairs and the food was served more or less all day. The mobile caterers did a fantastic job.

An interesting aspect of the indoor sequences was that Eric and Ernie could be seen playing out what really happens at a venue just before a show. They check the props, run through a gag or two and make sure the lighting is ready for the cue.

After the excitement of The Sweeney it was back to the hard work of churning out another series. Scripts had to be read and reread. New material to find or old material to modify, new jokes, new guests to find; the treadmill had started again.

Both of them were not getting any younger, and Eric's health again took a dive when he had his second heart attack in 1979. I knew he had been feeling ill a few weeks before, he had complained to me about bad indigestion, but I had thought no more about it. When I heard the news the first thing that came into my head was; "Oh no. Here we go again." It was a very worrying time for all concerned, and as I had been his driver and friend for over ten years at this point, it also affected me badly.

He was rushed into hospital and had a heart bypass operation that saved his life. After he was allowed home he was under very strict instructions not to work and to rest as much as he could. Under no circumstances was he to even consider working again for the next six months. This was Eric though, and he felt he had to be doing something. He couldn't relax, his mind was racing and he couldn't even go out birdwatching or fishing. Something else had to take the place of show business and that something was writing.

This still kept his mind occupied while allowing his body to rest, something that pleased Joan, his doctors and himself. He saw it as working; he still had to be creative, just not on stage or in front of the cameras. Writing was something he found he enjoyed tremendously, and he was writing about something he knew; being a comedian. The result of this burst of writing was seen a few years later when he released his first novel, Mr. Lonely. The story describes the life of a comedian from dank, backstreet clubs to fame and glory on television. A lot of material was pulled from his own experiences and some even claim it to be semi-autobiographical.

As time went on, he recovered enough for the doctors to allow him back to work. Together with Ernie and reunited with Eddie Braben, they set about getting back to normal again. Eddie's contract had expired during Eric's rest period and he was persuaded across to Thames to re-form the old team. The routines were not as energetic, the dance numbers were less and the rehearsal times were extended; all to help Eric. He wanted to work, he didn't want to let Ernie down and he didn't want to let the public down.

It was wonderful to see him back working with Ernie after such a long time away, but things were a little different. The heart attack seemed to throw both of them off a bit. Coupled with the new working methods at Thames meant the shows would have to be in a slightly different format, because of the adverts. Eddie's usually brilliant scripts had to be trimmed to fit a specific time and they even had to resort to reusing some of the BBC or ATV material. That's not to say it was all bad, some of the stuff equalled the BBC material, just there was less of it.

Writing for the best comedians in show business is no mean feat. Eddie had been doing it since 1969, and knew them probably better than themselves. Some writers can often struggle to make the connection with their stars and it often showed. Material that would be considered great for other comedians would seem flat and lifeless when given to Morecambe and Wise. For the material to shine it had to be written specifically for them by someone who knew how they worked from the inside; someone like Eddie. Having said that though, the well is not endless and even Eddie could struggle to be consistent, especially with the newly imposed time requirements.

Eric knew his health had taken a beating and was looking to slow things down, maybe even quit the never-ending television shows. He would not have packed it in completely and I know he would still do the Christmas shows with Ernie, but things were slowing down. He had found a new and more relaxing way to be creative with his writing and the hard work of the shows looked less tempting. I think his ideal position would be to write for most of the year, appear on panel or chat shows a few times and then do the Christmas show to finish things off.

As the years went on this became more apparent to me, but he would not let Ernie down. He would not give up on Ernie if he still wanted to perform and within the limits of his health this is what he did. Even an under par Morecambe and Wise show was good enough to top other shows at the time, but making them became tiring.

Thames kept up a steady schedule of around eight shows a year for the next few years, bringing in guests such as Max Bygraves, Hannah Gordon, Peter Bowles, Joanna Lumley, Richard Briers and Roy Castle to keep things interesting. Despite this everyone was feeling that they were just on a treadmill and they were producing nothing new. This ate away at Eric to the extent that he began to make plans to retire from the relentless procession of series after series.

The shows went down well enough with the public but never matched the BBC counterparts, and so with Eric as well as he could be, the work began on the promised film Night Train to Murder. It was to be a murder/mystery spoof with a host of famous people and Eric and Ernie right in the thick of it. Eric was particularly excited about the project and couldn't wait to get going.

He and Ernie contributed a lot of material for the film, but there were hold-ups and Eric soon got aggravated. He wished he had never started it, and when the final script came through, it seemed all of their material had been replaced by some other less talented ghostwriter. The budget was not as high as they had hoped and as a result it was filmed on standard VHS tape and not the normal film. It seemed everything was going wrong, but Eric persevered hoping that it would all come right in the editing room. How wrong he was. The finished film was so bad that he declared it should never be released.

I don't find the film terribly bad, just not funny and certainly not Morecambe and Wise. It had a few mildly entertaining segments like Eric trying to take off Ernie's shirt, and a few moving scenes, but nothing stood out and nothing seemed to gel. It was a rushed out, mixed up mess that bore no resemblance to the ideas Eric and Ernie had. Even the line up of well-known names like Fulton Mackay and Richard Vernon could not raise its profile, and it proved to be a very disappointing end to the partnership.

This was the last time Eric and Ernie worked together. After all the glory, the highs of the BBC, the twenty-eight million viewers, the live shows, to finish off with this must have hurt. Eric never talked about it; to him it was something that never happened.

Slowly Eric was getting back to his old self but in doing so was putting more pressure on his body and heart. No one knew just how much until 1984, in a small theatre in Tewkesbury.

Chapter 18 – Tewkesbury – The Beginning Of The End

Amongst the many venues I drove Eric to, the most enjoyable for him were the ones that offered different routes to them. If time allowed, he would often say, "Let's take the pretty route today." And we would set off taking in the beautiful views and often breathtaking scenery.

One such place was Tewkesbury. Surrounded by rolling countryside, whatever route you took, you were guaranteed some great views. On this particular day, 27th May 1984, we were both looking forward to having a peaceful drive as Eric was booked to play at The Roses Theatre. What neither of us knew though, was this beautiful day was to be his last. His last ride in his beloved Rolls, his last show, his last time on stage in front of an appreciative audience, his last day alive.

We drove through Redbourn, Kensworth, Whipsnade, Aylesbury and headed towards Oxford. On the other side of Oxford we passed Blenheim Palace, often used for the Lord's Taverners cricket matches, on through Woodstock, Chipping Norton, Stow-on-the-Wold and eventually to our destination, Tewkesbury.

Eric was excited about this event. It was his first real stab at a one-man show and one of the very rare occasions he would be on stage without Ernie. The whole thing came about because of his old friend and variety colleague, Stan Stennett. In the early days they had worked together on a regular basis as they toured the music halls and theatres of Britain. Once the variety days were killed off by the emergence of radio and television, they still kept in touch and became lifelong friends.

Stan had recently taken over The Roses Theatre and had asked Eric if he would like to do a one-man show to get things rolling for him. Because of Eric's health, there would be nothing strenuous, just a Question and Answer session, with Eric chatting to the audience about his life. Of course, with Eric involved, it could turn into anything, and if anything went wrong it would be funny. It would be Eric at his best, chatting with no script and the freedom to ad-lib as much as he wanted. He would also be in control. There would be no producer or director asking for retakes, no waiting for lighting or props, no one else to worry about, just him, a chair and the audience.

He was not at all nervous or worried before the show, he just sat back in the Rolls, relaxed and enjoyed the drive along with Joan, who came with him. Eric had been a bit under the weather just before the show and although not 100%, he hated letting anyone down, especially a good friend like Stan. We arrived in good time and quickly found our hotel and after unpacking the bags Eric decided he would like to take his customary walk and visit the theatre. He had never been to this one and was eager to see it, and just maybe a little bit of him wanted to make sure everything was prepared for him.

Eric and I set off and as soon as we walked in we both knew it was just right for him. It was one of those theatres that had been kept in its original condition; beautiful decor, small and intimate, and had that wonderful feeling that can't be explained. You just knew it was right. With the checks complete we both headed back to the hotel with Eric telling me that he would take a quick nap, but he would meet me for a cup of tea in half an hour or so. Eric sometimes had a nap before a performance. It was his way of relaxing and storing up energy, so I was not worried.

Sure enough, half an hour later, Joan, Eric and I set about a nice plate of cakes all washed down with the promised tea. As we were getting to the end of the cakes, Eric said he would like to take another stroll around. I think he just wanted to do something other than sit and wait for the show. By now the weather had changed and outside the pavements had a light covering of rain. Despite the thin drizzle, Eric and I set off, coats pulled tight, to have a mooch about and to check out the local shops.

He loved looking in shop windows, especially if it was a clock shop. A bit of a clock fan, he had a collection at home, and was always on the lookout for something special. Sadly, he found nothing, but I think he wasn't really looking. As the evening approached, we had agreed to meet Stan and his family at the theatre and as soon as we entered you could feel the buzz. Eric's face lit up, now he was really looking forward to it and couldn't wait to get started.

They had a quick run through with the band and it was arranged that after the first half variety show, Stan would introduce Eric and things would go from there. They planned to include the audience, allowing Eric to ad-lib when questions were asked, and to also be informative at the same time. It was like an interview in a way, but with the audience asking the questions. Should things dry up, Stan would be there to fill in with his own questions, but with Eric on stage the chances of that were remote to say the least. Eric insisted that he did not know the questions before hand, he wanted it to be spontaneous and for the audience not to think it was scripted.

With everything set, the audience began to file in and I took my place backstage as usual. Although there would be no handling of props, he somehow expected me to be there. The atmosphere was electric, and Eric asked me to check things out. No need to worry, I reported back, the place was packed with happy and excited fans.

The show excelled and was brilliant, even based on Eric's standards. Joan later commented that she wished someone had recorded it, as it was one of the most entertaining evenings of her life, at least for the vast majority of it. Eric was in dazzling form. The jokes and ad-libs flowed easily, he really relaxed and was enjoying himself out there. I think he was secretly a little bit relieved that he still had the magic; that he could still make people cry with laughter.

I was backstage, listening to the audience roar and cheer one minute, then be silent the next as Eric revealed a little but more about his life. The audience were lapping it up but as the show went on I could sense he was tiring. He was still in control, he had them in the palm of his hand and was loving every minute, but he was exhausted. Despite being ill and tired he kept on going; he wanted to give back some of the appreciation they had given him all night.

As the show neared what I hoped was the closing segment the band launched into a musical number, allowing Eric to quickly leave the stage. He came off and took the towel from me, wiped his face, took a sip of water, took a huge, deep breath and went straight back out again. It was at this point I began to worry about him. I kept saying to myself slow down, slow down.

Eric stayed on for another fifteen minutes, there on stage, in his element, in front of his fans. He must have come off and gone back on for an encore about six times. The last time he went back on he made for the drums and vibraphone. Sticks flying everywhere, he dug deep and pulled out some more energy. Trombone next, playing like a madman, audience coiled up with laughter. He was in stunning form, but getting weaker all the time. I could see it.

Finally he left the stage shouting, "That's all folks!" as he vanished from the audience's view. The applause was thunderous. A brilliant night, one of his best I thought, but I was still relieved he had managed to get off stage.

The next few words he said are etched into my mind forever. As he came off stage, he turned to me and sighed, "I'll have to pack this in. I'm getting too old for this."

He walked past me towards the dressing room, took a deep breath, let out a huge sigh and fell to the floor. It wasn't a sudden collapse; it all seemed to happen in slow motion, with me looking on totally helpless. Somehow he managed to hit his head on the way down and just lay there, in a heap on the floor.

I ran towards him, dropped down next to him and gently cradled his head in my hands; shouting for help as others came running. My worst fears had come true, another heart attack.

When Tommy Cooper died on national television, Eric had said what a terrible way to go and he would hate to go out like that. He had only just managed to avoid it. As I held him I could feel him breathing. My head was spinning and I began to doubt my own mind. Was he breathing? Was he alive? He is breathing, isn't he? I began to talk to him, trying to reassure him that everything was going to be fine and an ambulance would be here soon. I will never know if he heard me.

Holding his head was like holding something very fragile. I took the utmost care and just hoped someone with medical experience would get there soon. Luckily the mayor, also a doctor, arrived and quickly took over, leaving me and others to look on helplessly. My friend lay there, a few feet away being given the kiss of life and I was totally helpless.

Hold on Eric old friend. Hold on.

The ambulance arrived. Eric was moved into the back and Joan went with him.

We've had some good times pal, we can have many more, just hold on.

The ambulance set off for Cheltenham Hospital and I followed it every inch of the way in the Rolls. I wasn't going to let him out of my sight, not now. It was one of the longest and saddest journeys I've ever had to take. Still only a few feet away and still as helpless.

Stay with me Eric. I'm right here.

Once at the hospital it was more waiting. This time it was worse. I had nothing to keep me occupied, just a quiet room and my own thoughts. He can't die. Not Eric. This great, funny, talented, warm guy. He'd be all right. He'd pull through, he's a fighter. Boy did he put up a fight.

The medics worked on him for nearly four hours. He was hanging in there, but only just. At one point he actually squeezed the hand of a nurse as if to show total defiance of what was going on. He was fighting for his life, every step of the way. A fight that proved just too much.

Eric died around 4am in the morning. He never regained consciousness. The sunshine had gone.

Chapter 19 – On Stage

No one could have really known what it was like, there on that stage. How Eric felt, what thoughts were going through his mind and even if he realised that this would be his final appearance. I was in the wings so I was pretty close, but someone even closer was Alan Randall, the bandleader and pianist.

Alan Randall was renowned for his musical expertise the world over. Not only was he recognised and acknowledged as the premier recreator of George Formby's music and singing, but he was also Britain's foremost solo instrumentalist – a maestro of the vibraphone, ukulele and piano. He also appeared with Perry Como and Liza Minnelli in Las Vegas, and played in concerts with Sir Cliff Richard and The Rolling Stones. Add to this over 300 television appearances, 3,000 radio broadcasts and countless records, and it's not hard to see why he enjoyed a worldwide reputation for his musical skills.

Just before Alan died in 2005, he dictated his version of events that night to the Rev. Guy Bennett, as he had seen it, just a few feet away from Eric.

Initially he had met Eric years before on *Workers Playtime*, a popular radio show in the forties, fifties and sixties, but on this evening they were reacquainted in the car park of The Roses Theatre. He had arrived to set up the equipment for the band and was wearing a large black leather overcoat.

"Don't say you've brought your xylophone and set of drums on the back of a motorbike!" Eric quipped, friendly as always.

Later in the afternoon Alan arrived for the rehearsal and again bumped into Eric.

"I arrived for rehearsal during the afternoon," he recalled, "and Eric said, 'Where's your dressing room? I bet you haven't got one – you'd better come with me.' That was the sort of man Eric was – a household name, but there was no side to him."

"Anyway, in I go and we must have chatted for a couple of hours. He seemed as if he wanted to talk to me, mainly about the business, football and how he wanted to give up the pressure of work and semi-retire."

Alan didn't really think about it at the time, but here he was, in Eric's dressing room chatting about his future. Eric was a huge star and Alan, although very well-known in the world of music, still considered himself just a fan. He was honoured and too engrossed in Eric to actually think about what he was saying.

Later on, just before the show was due to start a waitress arrived and asked if they wanted anything from the bar, Eric just smiled and said he would love a big pot of tea. It duly arrived and they shared that last drink together before the show.

Alan notes how brilliant Eric was that night and how the audience were in stitches as he candidly, but comically, answered the questions posed by Stan Stennett. Eventually time caught up and the interval was called, and Eric came back to the dressing for another pot of tea – his last.

After the interval it was Alan's turn to take to the stage, firing up the orchestra and belting out some of the old classics. While he was going through the routines he could see Eric standing in the wings watching. Occasionally he would shout 'Go on lad, let 'em have it!' He was really enjoying it.

The last number was *The Entertainer* in honour of Eric and Alan was seated at the grand piano when suddenly Eric took to the stage. He sat down on the stool and started larking about, much to the audience's delight. Next came the drums, and Alan picked up a large bass drum and began to march up and down the stage, Eric was soon following him having grabbed another drum.

The vibraphone was next and the last instrument Alan had to play as the last few bars of the tune drew near. Eric followed him, eager to please and to squeeze every last laugh out of the routine.

"Which note do I play?" he asked Alan, who promptly pointed to the C and let Eric get on with it. With a flourish of notes, music and chaos the number finally ended. Eric smiling from ear to ear had the audience completely under his spell.

"Is that it then?" Eric asked as the music ended. The band struck up the walk off music and he approached the wings, flicking his glasses up and down. That was when Alan saw him fall.

He ran over to him and could see it was serious. The band were still playing and the audience clapping and there was Eric, collapsed on the floor.

An announcement was made, asking if there was a doctor in the audience and Joan turned to Alan's wife and immediately said, "It's Eric."

At 4am in the morning Stan called Alan to inform him that Eric had died.

Chapter 20 – Silence Is Not Golden

It was such a cruel end for such a nice man, and only 58 years-old. I am not sure if he would have liked to have gone out like that. He and Ernie had come through so much, strode on as others fell and kept their heads high even through the worst of times. Maybe he would have preferred a quieter moment. While fishing or privately with family.

I drove Joan home from the hospital in silence.

It seemed wrong somehow, that Eric wasn't there. Nothing was said, it was a sombre journey back to the family home. Joan sat staring into oblivion, by her side a carrier bag containing Eric's belongings. That trip seemed to never end, when it did I wished it hadn't.

We arrived back at the house around 11am and as we turned the corner the worst thing was there to greet us; the press. They were blocking the drive and it was obvious the news had broken and they were hungry for pictures and a story. They have a job to do, but when this kind of thing happens, the last thing you want to do is share the moment with the world.

We managed to crawl our way through the throng, flashlights bursting all around us until we struggled into the drive and past the gates. I pulled up to the front door and helped Joan out, quickly getting her into the safety of the house. I returned to the gates to close them and was immediately bombarded by questions and cameras. As soon as the gates were shut I returned to the house not knowing what the future might hold.

The old place was quieter now, and I sensed a sadness in those bricks. Something was missing and both Joan and I knew who it was.

As the funeral arrangements were made I offered to collect Eric from the hospital. I felt it was something I had to do. Not out of duty but out of friendship. Joan agreed it would be a nice gesture to bring him home just one more time. I took the Volvo estate and handled the task as though Eric was still alive. I would collect him and bring him back to his family. It was the only way I could make that trip.

As I arrived at the chapel of rest, I was asked if I would like to see him. I hadn't even considered seeing him again, but I took this opportunity to see my friend for the last time. I suddenly became very nervous. I don't know why, and to use one of Eric's sayings, hellfire! I knew this man. We had laughed together, dodged W.I. buses together, nearly set light to dressing rooms together, travelled the length and breadth of the country together, and we were friends, why should I be nervous!

I entered the room and closed the door behind me. Turning slowly around my gaze fell on my old friend, Eric Bartholomew. I can't say he looked well, he was dead, but he did look strangely happy. I know it sounds silly, but the stress had left him, the wrinkles were gone and he just looked, to use a cliché, at peace. His glasses, of course, were missing so nobody would recognise him should they enter the room.

With the help of the staff we dropped the seats of the Volvo down and slid the coffin into the car. Passenger in, and with a sad heart, I set off for the long journey home. My last ever journey with my friend, just the two of us, together for one final journey.

I had visions of being stopped by the police for some trivial reason and them noticing the coffin in the back. How can you explain that?

"And what is that in the back sir?"

"It's a coffin officer."

"Is it empty?"

"No, it's got Eric Morecambe in it."

I'm sure the press would have had a field day with that. They would have gone to town had they known that Eric was returning to his home in the back of his own Volvo. Eric would have seen the funny side, yet again he managed to give the press the slip.

Joan and the family were hit hard but amazingly it seemed the whole country was in mourning with them. I have never seen so much love and affection for a man. The news was awash with updates and the newspapers were flooded with good wishes from the public and celebrities alike.

The funeral was held in Harpenden Parish Church and the turnout would rival any Royal event. Hundreds and hundreds of people were there. People had travelled huge distances just to pay their respects; loyalty and indeed love. All ages seemed to be there, such was his appeal. All joined together, for once not to laugh, but to grieve together for their common loss.

Celebrities came too, you would expect it wouldn't you, but all eyes were on dear Ernie. Of all those affected, he surely must have been suffering the worst. He had known him longer than anyone, since they were young teenagers, and now he was here to say goodbye. Something very vivid happened that day; the touching of hands. As Ernie walked past people on his way to the church, people touched him very gently, to show they cared. Very, very gentle touches, fleeting, comforting taps. They knew he was hurting and wanted to ease the pain, but I don't think anyone could.

Floral tributes covered the ground, from football shapes to an amazing arrangement consisting entirely of sweet peas. The smell from those was wonderful and everyone commented on it and wondered who had sent it. I can tell you; it was from another great comic and admirer, Benny Hill. Although they had only met once, in the corridor at Thames, when two great people meet, there is an instant connection, especially in the comedy world.

As the day moved on, the crowds seemed to get bigger. It was a long, tiring, sad day that saw the world say goodbye to its favourite uncle, and my very good friend, Eric Morecambe.

Chapter 21 – After Eric

Joan, after the funeral, took on the remainder of Eric's appearances at various events, but as with all things, life slowed down to something near normal. I knew that before long my services would no longer be needed and in early 1985, I left my position and took employment elsewhere.

Eric will always be with me, as he will be for all those who loved him, and continue to love him now. I didn't realise how much I really missed my old friend until a short holiday in 1997. On our way to Butlins at Minehead, we passed a sign for Tewkesbury. Tears came to my eyes and a lump to my throat. The happy memories came flooding back and the sadness of that night in 1984. When you have known someone as special as Eric, you never forget.

I now live in Morecambe, a place that Eric and I used to visit on a regular basis, mainly to see his parents. I grew to like it and knew one day that I would like to live there.

The first time I actually drove him to this seaside town was before the M6 link, and it took around seven hours to get from Eric's home in Harpenden to Morecambe. Once the M6 link was completed that dropped to a more manageable four hours.

I can still remember Eric's father, George, sat chatting in the conservatory of Peacock Lane, Morecambe, telling stories from his past. Sadie refused to leave the area despite Eric offering to pay for them to move closer to Harpenden. In the end he bought them a lovely detached house in a nicer area, a happy medium. George recalled his poor childhood and how he and his own father would set up traps in the back garden. A dustbin lid would be propped up by a stick, and scraps of food were placed underneath. Tied to the stick would be a long piece of string that, given enough time, could be pulled to drop the lid and catch whatever was unlucky enough to be there. More often than not they caught starlings. This was not out of cruelty, but the need for a cheap meal. Yes, they actually ate starlings. Apparently they made lovely starling pies!

Morecambe drew me in, and along with my wife, I wanted to set up a bed and breakfast on the seafront. At the time there were also better schooling options for my two children, Steven born in 1983 and Sara born in 1987, and so we set about looking for the ideal property. Sadly we never found it. I was still determined to stay, so we rented a flat for a while, hoping that something would come along. Sure enough in 1990, we got news of a little newsagent's shop that was up for sale that contained a flat above it. Not exactly our B&B, but a start and our very own place in Morecambe.

The nearby power station brought in a lot of trade to the shop, which kept us going, but like all things, it came to an end with the closure of the station. This meant our trade vanished and again we found ourselves looking for another opportunity. I got a job in Lancaster with a security firm and briefly moved there to make things more convenient, all the time keeping our eyes to the sea and hoping for another break.

That break came in 1993, when a flat became available over a clothes shop, so back we moved, back to the salty air and the sea breeze. Contrary to what you are told, sea air is not always good for you, this was proven shortly afterwards in 1994 when I had to follow my old friend Eric and have a heart bypass operation. The operation went well and once I was fit enough to work, we got ourselves a little flat over a shop selling seashells and trinkets on the seafront. At the same time we noticed a lovely flat being renovated nearby and after some enquiries managed to get our foot in the door. Our foot was rapidly followed by the rest of us and our possessions; we had finally got the place we dreamed of.

As you know, Eric followed me back to Morecambe in 1999 in the form of the lovely and well-visited statue that now adorns the promenade; I can see him from my window every day. Sculptured by Graham Ibbeson, the larger than life statue was unveiled by the Queen on 23rd July 1999. What a day that was.

The whole seafront was packed and the area had to be cordoned off. Frank Finlay, Sir Robin Day and Eddie Braben were all there, as were Gary, Gail and their families; and of course Joan. The media were all over the place and finally the Queen would be coming to my place after the numerous visits I'd made to hers. I had never met her until this day, and it would happen in the large marquee that had been set up against all odds on the seafront. It should have been set up the day before, but due to bad weather, it had been delayed and so now, on the day of the unveiling, everyone was rushing about trying to get things tied down and secure.

I was interviewed twice by the television crews, and the whole place had a great atmosphere. As the Queen pulled off the sheet, there was a huge roar from the crowd, what a wonderful feeling. All those people there to see Eric, just like the old days. The statue sits on the promenade set against the backdrop of the Cumbrian hills, and when there is a spectacular sunset, it is truly breathtaking.

It seems regardless of the weather, someone will be there, posing for a photograph, recalling the jokes and routines; or just staring at him, remembering the laughter. To some it is almost a pilgrimage; they are here to visit an old friend, to be happy and away from the troubles of everyday life.

But what of the cars? Those beautiful machines of course didn't follow me here, I was just the driver. I have had the opportunity to catch up with them both over the years, and still get goosebumps when I sit in my seat. Both of Eric's Rolls Royces are, more or less, intact, albeit in very different states of repair.

His first one, a 1972 Rolls Royce Silver Shadow turned up in a scrapyard in Shrewsbury in 2009. It was saved from the crusher by Peter Yates, an eagle-eyed businessman who lives close to Morecambe.

He saved the old lady, brought her back to his garage and has fully restored her, ready to be hired out for special events. He came to visit me with the logbook to make sure it was original, and there was my signature, as clear as the day I signed it. He was originally planning something special in 2012 that will mark the 40-year anniversary of the car, which I was hoping to be involved with, but sadly it never happened.

The second 1974 Rolls, as I have already said, was bought at auction by three anonymous businessmen with the aim of, again, hiring it out. This car was recently rumoured to be back on the market, but nothing came of it. For those Morecambe and Wise fans that saw me driving a Rolls in a documentary, sadly it was not the original, it was a stunt Rolls with a fake number plate.

Very recently, in 2013, the whereabouts of the Jensen was also solved. This wonderful car has had a strange life after it left Eric. It had various modifications, was reregistered and eventually left to fall apart. Luckily, a Jensen fan purchased the remains and after tracking back the chassis number, discovered it was in fact Eric's old car. It is currently in Belgium being fully restored.

Away from Morecambe I still visit Harpenden now and again, some of the old shops are still there, many have gone. Eric loved the place, especially the variety of shops you could visit in a small area, the shops with character, unlike the large supermarkets of today. The fishing shop, the clock shop, the pipe shop, all sadly gone forever. Little islands of pleasure where you could browse the shelves for as long as you liked without being constantly badgered and asked if you needed help.

He could walk down the street and not be bothered by the people. They all knew him, but respected him and respected the fact that this was his personal time. They were there if he needed them, and sometimes he did. The time his Rolls broke down outside the supermarket and he got the staff to give him a push-start – only in Harpenden!

Despite my many moves and jobs since those joyous times, my

connection to Eric and of course Morecambe and Wise, has not lessened. The public still love them, and every year there seems to be something new happening to keep their names alive. Some of which I am involved with in one way or another. The Internet, not around of course back then, is a good place to find out things, and there are plenty of websites dedicated to Morecambe and Wise.

More recent news, in 2010, is that of the proposed Eric Morecambe museum, right here in Morecambe. What a wonderful idea, and let's hope the project gets the green light, I know Gary has been working hard on this project and has support from many quarters. It will be the ideal place to house Eric's belongings, including Charlie, the ventriloquist doll I looked after all those years will only be a few yards from my house. At least it won't be my job to repair and maintain it now.

Chapter 22 – A Star In My Own Lifetime

Being with Eric for over fifteen years, through the glorious BBC years and beyond, it was nearly always the case that a television camera would be close by. This was either to catch a brief glimpse of him in private or as part of an official engagement. It would therefore be prudent to assume with me driving him, I too may get my face on the screen, lurking under my hat somewhere in the background. This, in part at least, was true.

I was also given other opportunities to be included in several programmes both during his lifetime and after it. Call it my five minutes of fame, because if you add all of them up, you would probably get just short of the full five minutes. Somewhere, somebody owes me a few extra seconds.

My first big television role was to be in a documentary, filmed by the BBC in 1975. It was part of the Omnibus series and followed the making of a typical Morecambe and Wise show. Called *Fools Rush In*, I can be seen in all my splendour driving Eric to rehearsals. As I climb out of the car you can see my uniform in all its glory, including the nice hat mentioned so much in earlier chapters. For those eagle-eyed fans, the Rolls Royce I drive did not have the EM 100 number plate; the film was made just before we got that. The rehearsals were at Dalgarno Way, previously described in this book, and the director had specific duties for me. To me it was what I would normally do anyway, but I was asked to open the door, hand Eric his briefcase and leave. This I did to perfection, showing next to no acting skills at all. If you are keeping count by the way, that was about 30 seconds.

It all looked professional; me in my hat and Eric with his briefcase. The truth was, that was another prop and did not contain business documents, important contracts or scripts; no, instead it held his lunch and a newspaper.

Back to my acting career, if you can call it that, and we again go back to the seventies. This time my part was much more important, and came about due to a staff shortage rather than being planned or written. It was one Friday evening and the Morecambe and Wise show was currently in the process of recording the 'quickies'. Quickies were small, quick sketches that were shown to the audience in between Eric and Ern's live material. They padded out the show and for some reason often involved monks, particularly in the earlier shows. My role did not require me to wear any kind of robe, or luckily, shave my head.

This particular shot required a man in an ambulance uniform to hold one end of a stretcher. For some reason the actor either hadn't turned up or had been missed off from the cast list. Maybe he was made a better offer, whatever the reason; the production team were one man short. As they grouped together discussing possible ways around the problem, I stood off to one side, watching this unfold in my chauffeur's uniform. Unluckily they noticed me, or rather my uniform, and quickly seconded me to play the role. A tweak of the camera angle to try and hide the fact it was not an ambulance man and the scene was shot.

As I watched the broadcast, waiting for my big screen moment, all that was visible was my hat and nose, tucked away at the edge of the screen. For some reason I have only ever seen this once and have yet to see it on the DVD releases. Maybe my hat and acting skills were upstaging the boys; at least it brought my on-screen count to one minute.

Any fan of Morecambe and Wise will be aware of the numerous documentaries made about them, usually with other stars giving their opinions and experiences. There have been several that I have been asked to participate in too.

'Heart and Soul of Eric Morecambe' was one such documentary and required me to drive a Rolls Royce up and down Morecambe seafront. It wasn't Eric's car; it was just another Rolls of the same colour with EM 100 number plates stuck on. Still, I enjoyed providing these 'continuity shots' and it brought back happy memories. Lesley and I got to go to the then unrestored Midland Hotel to do further filming, adding our comments and thoughts about my dear friend. This wonderful hotel has since been fully restored by Urban Splash and is well worth a visit if you are ever in the area. That amounted to nearly a full minute; my total was rising fast.

Continuing with documentaries, and another interview that required my immense and growing acting abilities. The Unforgettable Eric Morecambe, broadcast in 2001, was another celebrity-laden look at the life and work of Eric. I got my airtime, but what you are not made aware of is how much work went into my short appearance. I suppose it is the same with anything of this kind, a camera is pointed in your direction and someone asks a lot of questions. As you answer, they nod, read from a clipboard and continue until they run out of questions, the camera breaks or one of us falls asleep.

I was there for over an hour, answering all the questions to the best of my ability, but it seems my question answering prowess may not be as good as my acting or driving; they broadcast about two minutes of it bring my grand total to four minutes.

As I recall, much the same thing happened in another lesser-known documentary called Local Heroes. For that they filmed me in my home, next to a window with lovely views out across Morecambe Bay. Another long filming session cut down to about 30 seconds; damn, just short of my allotted five minutes!

Television is only part of my media portfolio though; from television we move sideways to other formats. Whenever anything connected with Eric happens around Morecambe, the phone rings and on the other end will be the local newspaper, The Visitor, or BBC Northwest, sometimes even Granada News. The events covered by this generic catch-all included, and began with, the original unveiling of the statue in Morecambe in 1999. My radio experience continues to this day, my opinion and comments broadcast on subjects such as the 2009 anniversary of the statue, the museum, the Winter Gardens and even football.

I was also called into action when the second Rolls was bought by Snowden & Partners in 2006, when the first Rolls was found recently in 2009 and when Gary turned up to research his book the same year.

In 2008 Stagecoach launched the Morecambe & Wise bus that was on active duty around the area. There was a lovely launch party at the Midland Hotel and to see the bright yellow bus driving past, emblazoned with images of my friend, always brings a smile.

In September 2012 I was asked to participate in a very special reunion. Joan and Gary were visiting Morecambe, and for Joan it was her first trip since the statue was unveiled in 1999. As a surprise, Gary had asked if I could bring the newly restored Rolls to meet her and I gladly accepted. It was a trip down memory lane for both Joan and myself, and quite emotional too. She had not seen the car since it was sold in 1974, and now, after a very impressive restoration, it gleamed in the sun just like it did when I used to clean it.

Together all three of us drove around the area visiting places Joan had expressed an interest in, some, like the Winter Gardens theatre, to see the work being done inside, others of a more personal nature.

We visited Carnforth station, where the cinematic great *Brief Encounter* was filmed, and had tea in the tea rooms that replicate the ones in the film. There is also a mini museum there, dedicated to steam travel. It was a wonderful experience to be driving Joan again, in the original car, but something told me there was someone missing.

I was again back at Carnforth in July 2013 to help raise money for charity. The Northern Belle train, sister to the Orient Express, had done a run from Manchester to Carnforth for the charity '*When You Wish Upon A Star*' that raises money for sick children. Four people on board (Richard and Julie Want, Neil and Janine Martin) had won an auction, again for charity, and the prize was something called 'A

Brief Encounter with Eric.'

The title had double meaning, and they were in for a real treat. Things started in the tea rooms with complimentary food provided by the proprietors Andrew and Helen Coates. After this I drove them from the station to Morecambe in the Rolls. The car has been christened 'Eric' by Peter Yates, so that was the first meaning out of the way. The trip took us around Morecambe and the stomping ground of Eric, neatly tying up the other.

The tour took in most of the buildings and places linked to Eric (the person) with the exception of Morecambe Town football ground, which has sadly now been demolished and a new one built some distance away from the original site close to his old home in Christie Avenue.

The Morecambe Winter Gardens theatre was the next stop, and a free tour around the wonderful Victorian building that is still being renovated after having been saved from demolition by Evelyn Archer and a group of people who became known as 'the Friends of the Winter Gardens'.

The last treat, before heading back to Carnforth for more snacks and drinks, was a drive along the promenade at Morecambe, finishing at the statue of the town's favourite son, and my old mate Eric. It's great to see him (in one form or another) still raising money for charities nearly 30 years after his death.

Another visit to the area, this time by Eric's daughter Gail in October 2012 saw me acting as tour guide and driver again, sadly not in the Rolls this time. Gail was here to open a new bird hide at RSPB Leighton Moss, named after her father. The first one was originally opened by Joan 28 years ago, and had finally succumbed to the elements.

The list goes on, but I have to stop somewhere, and I'm sure you get the picture by now.

It is however wonderful that Eric is still in the hearts of so many people, and knowing him in person and as a friend, may he long continue to be remembered.

With or without new projects, books and films, I still look back on my time with Eric as the best time in my life. There were so many little things that it seems every object I see now has a little story. Quick glimpses back to happy times, moments that have passed in the blink of an eye remain with me. Events and happenings that spring to mind, triggered by every day conversations, that are buried deep inside me. I couldn't recall them until something or someone caused a little flag to wave and the memories, like old toys from your childhood toy box, climb out and just for a little while, take you back to a happier time. Some, the ones that I can remember in detail are in this book; some are more personal and some like the ones that follow don't quite fit into any category but like the one-liners Eric used to throw about, are small, perfectly formed, and always bring a smile.

Chapter 23 – Looking Back

Looking back over the 14 years I knew and worked for Eric, there are many moments I shall never forget, most you have read about and shared in this very book. Some, though, only spring to mind at certain times, triggered perhaps by something I see or hear, or something someone says. They don't even have to be talking to me, which is quite common these days.

I recently heard the sad news that Jim Bowen has had a stroke and even this sad news brought back another hidden memory. Eric and I were in Morecambe, it was 1981 and he had decided he wanted to go for a quiet drink. Although run down at the time, his first choice was the Midland hotel, he could usually go unnoticed in there, which on this particular day he wanted. We drove there in the Rolls and headed towards the cocktail bar. As we entered I noticed Jim was stood at the bar with his back to us, I pointed him out to Eric who went across.

"Hello sunshine," Eric said, joining him at the bar.

Bullseye, Jim's new show had just finished its first series and the critics were having a witch-hunt. They panned it leaving Jim a bit dejected and considering his next career move. He had gone out for a quiet drink and the last thing he expected or at the moment needed, was Eric to arrive asking him if he had read the newspapers.

Eric put a positive spin on it though, reminding him that the hardest thing to find is yesterday's newspaper. He came back to our table and Eric told him about how he and Ernie went through the same thing with Running Wild. That show really got hammered but to beat it they just kept working.

Eventually, he told Jim, the press will move on to their next target and you'll wonder what all the fuss was about. In some ways I think Eric helped Jim get over that initial shock, and gave him a much needed confidence boost.

You would think that working for Eric might be the best job in the world, which for the most part was true, but there was still the 'real' work to contend with.

Cleaning the swimming pool, walking the dog and mowing the lawn; there was a lot of lawn to mow, I can certainly vouch for that. Those though, were outweighed by the glorious times, the times of meeting other famous people, getting into places I could have only dreamed about and of course, wearing a nice hat.

I have wonderful memories of meeting Bruce Forsyth and his then wife, Anthea. I pulled up into his impressive driveway, alongside his large house that overlooked a golf course. The entrance hall was massive, with a glittering chandelier hanging from the ceiling. We ate in his opulent kitchen, enjoying the nice food and non-alcoholic drinks.

In a time before mobile phones, if I wasn't invited along, we had to rely on arranged times. I would drop Eric off and call back to collect him at the time he specified. Sometimes he would stay a little longer if the company was good, which obviously meant I had to wait as well. The times I was invited in though, are the times I remember best.

I was very kindly invited into Dame Judi Dench's home and met her husband Michael Williams. We had lunch in her beautiful cottage in Hampstead, which I believe has been very badly damaged by fire since. Eric was like part of the family, just as he was with television viewers. People loved to meet him, to invite him in and to feed him and to listen to his stories and anecdotes.

Many of the famous people I encountered were usually passengers though. I drove Michael Crawford to a social event, another nice person, and I even managed to get into the Houses of Parliament for a quick brew.

Of the people I actually met that were more than just passengers I recall happy memories of John Alderton and Pauline Collins, Ronnie Barker and his wonderful saucy postcard collection, Bernie Winters, a brief encounter with Frankie Howerd and the kindness of John Inman. Many short, often fragmented stories that involve flash meetings with celebrities that probably meant very little to them but to me it was another memory of the time I spent with Eric.

As you meet other drivers, some become familiar and you always nod or have a quick chat during the minutes your employer is elsewhere. One driver I knew often crossed my path; a driver of peers. He would ferry politicians and lords around London, and so I got to see him whenever Eric was there. One particular lunchtime we were together and because of who he worked for, he had a pass to the canteen inside the Houses of Parliament. With a nod and wink, we both strolled past the policemen and parliament staff and straight into the canteen. It wasn't really allowed, but once inside, and seeing the subsidised prices, my quick brew changed into a three-course meal.

It was one of those unexpected events that littered my life during that period, and was something that I grew to love. Just working and being with Eric more or less guaranteed something out of the ordinary would happen. Sometimes it was hilarious; sometimes it was scary and sometimes just plain embarrassing.

I will admit, finally, here in print, that I once wore tights. There, it's out, and as my dear friend would say; there's no answer to that. It was all for a good cause of course, but embarrassing nonetheless.

It was a charity event at the Lakeside Club in Frimley Green and attending would be Princess Anne. Some fool thought it would be a good idea to have two footmen to greet guests as they arrived and so Eric and Ernie's agent got one of their employees and myself to fill in. Before the event I had to go to get my costume. It was the full regalia, tights, buckled shoes, everything. To be honest I wasn't looking forward to it, but the end result was fantastic and a great deal of fun.

A different man looked back at me from the mirror. I have no idea who he was, but he had great legs. Even Eric asked him out, twice, both times he was declined – Ernie had asked first. Who could blame them though, fancy clothes, black tights and a curly black wig – I think that's what interested Ernie. Later at the dress rehearsals all went well despite the numerous advances from various members of the band. Peters and Lee, a popular singing duo was to do the first half with Eric and Ernie finishing off for the second. Like all of their live shows, it went extremely well, and even the footmen got to go on the stage at the end to take a bow. We even met Princess Anne at the end, and me wearing tights too!

You can't analyse someone like Eric; better people than me have tried and fallen flat on their faces. All I can say is that he was the funniest, most natural comic I have ever had the privilege to know or meet. In many ways he was like that other comic great, and Eric's friend, Tommy Cooper. He only had to walk on stage and people would start giggling. It is a great gift that Eric used in abundance and without expectation of getting anything back. He went to great lengths to get a laugh; he wrote, rehearsed, rewrote, ad-libbed and rehearsed again until he was happy that he could make it no better. Then and only then would it be good enough for the public.

The shows themselves hold a lot of memories, especially the ones that I had the privilege of seeing the whole thing through from the start. In one of them, the great Shakespearian actor Ralph Richardson had agreed to appear. Eric couldn't believe it. This was a well-renowned classical actor, coming on to the show and opening himself up for the torrent of gags that would inevitably get thrown at him. As it turned out, he had never even seen a Morecambe and Wise show, and so had no idea what to expect. He also had no idea about the lines he was given, he had never heard, "Tea Ern," or "You can't see the join." They meant absolutely nothing to him.

The audience was in stitches as the gags began to flow, but he just stood there with this bewildered look on his face, which made it even funnier. Later in the show, for the ending, he was given a paper bag, but again had no idea why. He set about trying to swat imaginary flies with it, for reasons only known to himself.

Eric laughed at that moment, but he was not a stranger to odd behaviour. Away from the crowds Eric had his own strange quirks that seemed to amuse him for no reason I can fathom. There were times he would suddenly get an urge, I have no idea where from, and just do the oddest things. He had one strange habit that he later took up as a kind of game.

Usually the urge took him while out on the street; this is where it worked best although I suppose it could work anywhere. He would be walking along and then suddenly stop. He would tilt his head back and gaze upward, staring at something skyward. He would stay like that for a few minutes until someone would recognise him. They approached him but because he was obviously doing something, they didn't speak. Instead they looked up trying to see what was taking Eric's attention. Eric would just keep looking up without blinking, a puzzled look on his face. The passer-by would look harder, desperately trying to see this important thing that Eric was staring at. Eventually, unable to see anything, they would have to say something.

"Erm, excuse me, what are you looking at?"

Eric would look at them and put his hands in his pockets.

"Oh yes." He would say, and walk off.

This left the other person completely confused and totally bewildered; not knowing what had just happened or what to do next. They usually took a sneaky look up, just to check there wasn't actually anything there before leaving quietly, Eric, out of earshot, would mumble, "One...". That would be the first of the day, with many more to follow.

Those are the things that I miss. The madness, the genius, the feeling of being in the presence of someone like Eric. The strongest impression I have of him was his enthusiasm and ability to mix with anyone. It didn't matter if they were famous people, lords, royalty, miners, grannies or children, he could mix with them all, and they all came away smiling. He would put himself out to make sure he met everyone he could. He was almost humbled by the fans because he knew that if it weren't for them, he wouldn't be where he was. And just look at where he was. It wasn't bad for a lad that came from a council estate, worked down a coal mine and got rejected so many times from theatres and radio.

It was this hard journey I think, that made Eric Morecambe who he was, that and a razor-sharp mind honed from years of treading the boards. He worked hard, and that meant that I had to too. One example was a charity event in Jersey; it would be a hectic couple of days and a typical weekend in the busy life of Eric Morecambe.

Remember, they were not getting paid for this; it was all part of keeping them in the public eye, and of course doing their bit for charity.

Friday would be the packing day. Not just clothes but props, make-up and the bits needed for the show they had agreed to do for Sir Billy Butlin. Was it all there, did it all work, where was that paper bag, had anyone seen Charlie's wig? Once everything was in order it was off to bed ready for the morning. Up early, Eric, Joan and I drove to Heathrow Airport where we met up with Ernie and his wife Doreen. Also there were other people taking part like Frankie Vaughan and of course the band headed by musical director Johnny Wiltshire.

Sir Billy had organised a chartered flight for all participants in the London area, and for me this was the first time I had flown. We got to Jersey and the afternoon was spent rehearsing and setting up the props for the show. Johnny was organising the band and working with Eric and Ernie to get the musical cues right. He and the band were with Morecambe and Wise for all of their live shows during the seventies, so knew how things worked.

A few hours rest and then came the show itself, which went down very well. As the crowds headed off home, we still had to pack everything back up and we had finally finished around 3am. A few hours sleep and then back to it. Packing the gear into the transport, back to the airport for the flight to Heathrow. Back in London and the gear was stacked back in the cars and I drove us all back home.

Despite the heavy schedules, both Eric and Ernie would always try to fit in charity events; it was as if they couldn't say no. I often get these flashbacks barging through my head, causing me to stop and remember the good old days and the madness of it all.

During the initial publicity for Eric and Ernie's first autobiography, the publishers had arranged many book signings up and down the country. At this time Morecambe and Wise were huge, and the crowds that came along were staggering. Imagine having to drive through several thousand screaming people; it was their own fault, they should have moved their feet! But seriously several thousand is a tremendously scary amount of people to find yourself in the middle of, especially when they all want to get inside your car.

Even something simple like opening a new supermarket drew thousands of people if Eric and Ernie were there. Once in Essex so many fans turned up that the place came to a standstill and we had to call for a police escort just to get us to the supermarket. Those scary moments were few and far between though, outnumbered by the masses of little moments that never fail to bring a little chuckle to my face.

The times Eric appeared in those oversized safari shorts with his thin legs dangling beneath and sock suspenders. That bemused look on his face and a glint in his eye. You can tell when someone is on top form from that look they get, they seem to be on another plane, and Eric had it almost constantly while he was healthy. That cheeky sparkle, the quick look sideways, the wry smile that told you something brilliant was about to happen. There were times he didn't even have to do anything, but just walk on dressed in an outrageous costume as though it was the most normal thing in the world.

Take the Jungle Book routine from the Thames Christmas show 1979. Because Eric was still recovering from his second heart attack, it was one of the very few things he did that year, but boy did he enjoy it. The show was more of a chat show than a full seasonal special and was hosted by David Frost. Eric and Ernie, after a little crosstalk introduction, settled down and talked about their careers in front of a studio audience. At intervals in-between the talking, a few short sketches were shown that they both managed to do; the Jungle Book being one of them.

Props of any kind always thrilled Eric, and the suit he was given was no exception. It was a full body Baloo bear suit, designed to give the impression of short legs; it is very difficult to describe unless you have seen it. The end result, combined with Eric's fluid movement and expressions was brilliant. He used that suit like a ventriloquist uses a dummy, it was part of him and he used it to its full potential. Dancing through the full song 'I Wanna Be Like You', it was hot and tiring, but well worth the effort.

There are also visions of Eric away from the television and fans that stay with me. The times when he was going fishing and looked genuinely happy to be on his own, almost relieved to get away. The times at home with his fish, his books and of course his family.

Eric is never far from my thoughts, whether it be on television in a repeat, in a book on my bookshelf or on a DVD sat beneath my television. My home has his pictures on the walls and now retired I have the luxury of being able to recall these wonderful memories. Most happy, some sad, some desperately heartbreaking, but I wouldn't trade them for anything.

The one persistent thing that always seems to appear though is Tewkesbury, and I ask myself the same question every time, why? Why did he do six encores? Why did he ignore the doctor's advice to rest? Why did he think he was letting anyone down by not doing it? I suppose I never will know.

What I do know is that I remember with pride, love and respect, the times I spent with Eric. The times I drove him, the times we chatted and the times we laughed. It was a privilege and an honour to have known him. The lovely thing is, I can look out of my window anytime and see him, still giving pleasure to many visitors and fans.

He will always be with me.

Acknowledgements

We would like to thank the following people without whom this book would never have been complete.

Lesley Fountain	Wife and mother to Steven and Sara.
Vi Chapman	Lesley's mother.
Gary Morecambe	For friendship, foreword and help with this book.
Gail Stuart	For her foreword and kind assistance.
Gideon Chilton	For support and encouragement and sandwich eating.
Stephen Mansfield	Endless proofreading, suggestions and ideas.
Sue Catling	Endless proofreading, suggestions and ideas.

Photograph Acknowledgements

Suzanne Simpkin	Hannah Gordon and Hugh Paddick photograph.
Nigel Dodinson	Two photographs (70s publicity event).
Paul Jenkinson	Morecambe and Wise bus. Michael at the statue. Rolls in garage.
Sophie Milward	Noele Gordon photograph
Michael Ingram	Knorr corporate film photograph.
Mercury House Pubs.	Practical Gardening magazine.
Ann Martin	Phyllis Dixey photograph.
Pieter-Jan Baert	Jensen Interceptor photograph.
Robert Swan	Eric waves to Eric.
Michael Fountain	All other photographs.

Thanks

We would like to thank and mention the following people:
Joan Morecambe, Doreen Wise, Jayne Chilton, Robyn Chilton, Elliot Chilton, Georgina Chilton,
Barbara and Raymond Jenkinson, Peter Yates, Joan Yates, Ernest Maxim, Eddie Braben, John Ammonds, Ann Hamilton and Dave Miles for early encouragement and finally Hyla and Connie Fountain without whom there would be no me!

Other Resources

If you are a fan of Morecambe and Wise, or want to find out more information, visit:
www.morecambeandwise.com

Other Reading

Morecambe and Wise by Graham McCann. ISBN: 1857027353
Morecambe and Wise Untold by William Cook. ISBN: 0007247966
Morecambe and Wise: Behind the Sunshine by Gary Morecambe and Martin Sterling. ISBN: 0330341405
The Book What I Wrote by Eddie Braben. ISBN: 0340833734